Shaping the education of slow learners

Special needs in education

SERIES EDITOR

Ron Gulliford, Senior Lecturer in Education,
University of Birmingham

Shaping the education of slow learners

W. K. Brennan
Assistant Education Officer for Special Education,
Inner London Education Authority

Routledge & Kegan Paul
London and Boston

First published in 1974
by Routledge & Kegan Paul Ltd
Broadway House, 68-74 Carter Lane,
London EC4V 5EL and
9 Park Street,
Boston, Mass. 02108, USA
Set in Linotype Baskerville
and printed in Great Britain by
Northumberland Press Limited, Gateshead
© W. K. Brennan 1974

ISBN 0 7100 7984 2 (C)
      0 7100 7985 0 (P)

Contents

Series editor's preface

This series of books on special educational needs will be concerned with the practice of special and remedial education whether in ordinary or special schools, with the findings and implications of research and with the discussion of organization and provision. The series aims to provide informed accounts of the needs of different groups of handicapped pupils and how these needs may be met by appropriate teaching, therapy and care.

Shaping the education of slow learners is concerned with the largest group of pupils needing special educational help; a group which includes pupils very varied in ability, personal and social characteristics. Although there has been a steady increase in the amount of special school provision, and progress has been made in various forms of remedial education, it must be admitted that we have not really got to grips with the problem of educating the 15 per cent or so of pupils who are the least able and successful in our schools. There are conflicting views about whether these pupils have different curricular needs from other pupils; there is uncertainty about how far they can be educated alongside other children or should have special classes and other special forms of organization; there is a shortage of teachers who are interested, trained and experienced for this kind of teaching.

It has not been Mr Brennan's aim to come up with ready-made solutions but to provide a basis of ideas and information for the discussion of aims and objectives. He examines the

vii

development of concepts about backwardness; the characteristics and needs of slow learners; the teaching approaches which have grown out of practical experiences; the implications of studies of the post-school progress of slow learners; the impact of recent curricular developments. He makes some positive proposals for classifying the needs of slow learners, distinguishes different kinds of special teaching and suggests some interesting priorities in curriculum planning. The book will prove a valuable basis for much-needed discussion of what we ought to be aiming to achieve in the education of slow learners.

Ron Gulliford

Preface

This book brings together the results of research and teaching experience with slow learners, suggesting, on the basis of these, a new way of categorizing their educational needs which should assist teachers in developing curricula relevant to those needs. Throughout, the discussion is related to the education of slow learners in the ordinary school where, rightly, the majority of slow learners will receive their education. First, the responsibility of the ordinary school is defined. Then, successively, characteristics of slow learners are reviewed and reorganized in a way related to education; knowledge of the post-school experience of slow learners is summarized and related to the school curriculum; literature on the curriculum for slow learners is reviewed and a plan for the continuous development of curricula is outlined in a way consistent with the modern approach to curriculum development. The object is not to inform teachers of what they must do: it is to assist them to think about their role as teachers of slow learners with more definite purpose so that their work may be enriched, and through it the education of their pupils. Throughout, it is assumed that those who elect to work with slow learners will relate to pupils warmly and be sensitive to their needs, hence the discussion concentrates on the more neglected, but not less important, technical aspects of the teacher's work.

Experienced, practical teachers should find the book adds richness to their background knowledge. Teachers on advanced courses in special education will find that the book is a useful introduction and continuous guide to the essential literature on the education of slow learners.

Many colleagues have contributed, indirectly, to this book but I acknowledge my special debt to my teachers in special education, R. Gulliford and A. E. Tansley, and to my former colleague in the Cambridge Institute of Education, Mrs K. F. Devereux.

W. K. Brennan

The author is Assistant Education Officer, Special Education, with the Inner London Education Authority and also Director of a Schools Council Project on the Curricular Needs of Slow-Learning Pupils. Neither the ILEA nor the Schools Council is in any way responsible for the content of this book.

1 Slow learners: a responsibility of the ordinary school

Who are the slow learners?

This is the description of a *typical* boy taken from a study of forty backward boys in the first year of their secondary schools (C. Jones, 1970):

He is 11·4 years of age with a mental age of 9·7 and a reading age of 7·4 years. He has established a basic sight vocabulary, has learned the sounds of most letters but has difficulty with consonantal and vowel diagraphs in that order. He has an even chance of being right handed and right eyed but failing this is likely to be right handed and left eyed. He has no major difficulty in form perception though he may show weakness in hand–eye co-ordination, the copying of simple forms and in visual rhythm, the ability to recognize and complete a regular visual pattern. In copying he tends to rotate his paper in order to draw a horizontal line in the vertical plane.

This typical boy lives in a council house; he is the third child in a family of four or five children; he shares a bedroom but has his own bed. He is the son of a semi-skilled or unskilled manual worker and he receives 15–20p to spend each week. There is a one-in-four chance that the boy's home is disturbed, with parents either separated or divorced.

Generally the boy has good health, but if he has a physical weakness it is likely to be poor eyesight. His school attendance is good and he shows average eagerness to learn in his new school. On the whole he mixes easily with his form mates, though he tends to form special friendships with a few of his own age and in conversation with them uses sentences which are short and simple in structure. In his school behaviour he shows reasonable persistence and independence, but should he have an extreme tendency it will be towards timidity and he may not quite have outgrown tale-telling and attention seeking.

Many teachers of slow learners will be able to put names to this description from the pupils in their classes. It remains, now, for us to look in more detail for the answer to the question: who are the slow learners?

Since its use by Tansley and Gulliford (1960), the term 'slow learner' has been increasingly used in reference to pupils who are failing in their school work. It is used in this sense by the Department of Education and Science (1964) to indicate 'children of any degree of ability who are unable to do work commonly done by children of their age', and the use of the term is regarded as interchangeable with the term 'backwardness'. A. A. Williams (1970) accepts the term slow learner but restricts its use to 'those children who are of limited intelligence', and he specifically excludes the 'erratic but underfunctioning child of high potential' (p. 9). Gulliford (1969) also makes use of the term, but he appears to exclude from it 'retarded children', defined by him as 'of average or good intelligence', but with a 'marked discrepancy between their educational achievements and their ability as judged by intelligence tests or their general performance in everyday affairs or non-academic aspects of schooling' (13). Gulliford also suggests that the slow learner is a pupil in an ordinary school rather than in a special school and in discussion he holds the category 'slow learner' distinct from that of 'educationally subnormal'. In contrast with this, Bell (1970) takes a view more consistent with that of A. A. Williams (1970) and regards 'slow learner' as interchangeable with 'educationally subnormal', 'backward' or 'less able'. The Plowden Report (DES, 1967a) recommended that the term 'slow learner' should be substituted for 'educationally subnormal' mainly on the grounds that the latter caused 'unnecessary distress to parents', a point also suggested by A. A. Williams (1970) who notes the 'condemnatory overtones' attaching to 'educational subnormality'. P. Williams (1970) comments that 'Regrettably, any term used to describe our slow responders seems in time to acquire its own odium, and a quarter of a century seems to represent the limit of its useful life' (p. 472). Nevertheless he accepts the term slow learner in general but is careful to exclude from his discussion the extreme cases of slow learners, those children who are receiving their education in special schools for severely ESN pupils (the former Junior Training Centres) or in hospitals for the subnormal. He regards such pupils as having very acute, special learning problems which justify describing and treating them separately from the rest of the slow learners whose intelligence levels are higher and who are found in special ESN schools and in special classes in the ordinary schools (Williams and Gruber, 1967).

At this point it may be helpful to look somewhat more closely at the term 'educational subnormality' which has intruded into the above discussion of the slow learner. Educationally subnormal pupils are defined in *Handicapped Pupils and School Health Regulations* (Ministry of Education, 1959) as 'pupils who, by reason of limited ability or other conditions resulting in educational retardation, require some specialized form of education wholly or partly in place of the education normally given in ordinary schools'. There are points about the definition which should be carefully noted by teachers. It is a definition which does not rely exclusively upon the results of intelligence tests but allows for consideration of many other factors which influence educational progress; it does not imply that special education must be given in a special school or on a full-time basis but allows provision within the ordinary school and for part of the curriculum only, where such arrangements meet the needs of the pupils. In the best sense the definition is *educational*, for it is based upon the response of the pupil in learning situations and it emphasizes the importance of modifying the learning situations to meet the needs of the pupil. Indeed, most educationally subnormal pupils are *discovered by their*

3

teachers in the schools and put forward for examination by psychologists and school medical officers who should be concerned with eliciting psychological or medical *causes* for the pupil's failure to learn, which might be helpful to those who must *teach him*. Merely to confirm what the school knows – that the pupil is educationally subnormal – is to misuse the opportunity presented by the examination and is usually considered unhelpful by experienced teachers. The fact is that most educationally subnormal pupils in ordinary schools are unlikely to have received any special psychological or medical examination which could have added to their teachers' knowledge and through that to the quality of their education.

In the sense that either may be used to indicate a pupil who is unable to cope with school work normal for his age, 'educationally subnormal' and 'slow learner' are interchangeable terms. But both suffer from serious limitations. One limitation is that for full meaning both terms must be seen in the framework of the definitions of other categories of handicapped pupils: blind, partially sighted, deaf, partially hearing, epileptic, maladjusted, physically handicapped, pupils with defective speech and delicate pupils (ibid.). Any of these handicaps may result in a pupil being unable to cope with school work normal for his age, but where such failure is clearly a consequence of the primary handicap, the education of the pupil is usually organized in ways suitable for that handicap. Where the relationship between primary handicap and educational failure is not clear, or where the latter is sufficiently grave to require special education even in the absence of a primary handicap, then decisions about the education of the pupil require considerable, experienced and informed judgment based upon high-quality educational, social, psychological and medical information. Another limitation is that both 'slow learner' and 'educationally subnormal' are general terms which *label* a condition of educational failure without either indicating or explaining its nature or causation. The acceptance of either term as a unitary explanation may encourage unjustified generalizations about 'educationally subnormal children' or 'slow-learning children' which divert attention from the variety and multiplicity of causes operating in cases of school failure, with consequent stereotyping of educational provision and treatment.

There is, in fact, growing dissatisfaction with the definition of educational subnormality, and with the other definitions of handicapping conditions noted above. This is not surprising if it is remembered that the definitions were formulated in the late 1940s and are based upon the thinking of the 1930s. Since that time there has been considerable change in social conditions; development and improvement in the educational system itself; radical changes in our concepts of intellectual development and the nature of intelligence; new knowledge and growing experience about the teaching and learning of backward children. Indeed, the very substitution of the term 'slow learner' for 'educationally subnormal' is part of the growing criticism of the current definition. We shall return to this in the next chapter, but in order to further the present discussion an attempt must be made to formulate an answer to the question posed above: Who are the slow learners?

Definition of the slow learner

Slow learners are regarded as those pupils who are unable to cope with the school work normal for their age-group but whose failure cannot be explained by the presence of any handicapping condition defined in the ten categories of handicapped children. Should any such condition be present in a pupil who is to be regarded as a slow learner, then it will be in marginal form only and clearly secondary to the learning difficulty which is the primary cause of school failure. Such slow learners will not exhibit severe intellectual retardation which might cause them to be considered as suitable for education in schools for mentally handicapped pupils (the former Junior Training Centres) or in hospitals for the mentally subnormal; nor will they exhibit above-average intellectual ability combined with their learning failure. On the positive side these slow learners will use speech to communicate (albeit at a retarded level) and they will relate to other persons in a normal manner, though they may show some immaturity or insecurity resulting from their experience of failure. As so defined, slow learners overlap from the special (ESN) schools, where they are the most able pupils in the higher ranges of intelligence, to the classes for backward pupils in ordinary schools where they form the majority of those pupils.

The above definition of slow-learning pupils is consistent with the recommendation of the Plowden Committee and takes account of the reservations of many of the writers discussed above. It is still a 'general' definition, with all the dangers noted above, and it must be retained at that level in order to discuss the size of the population of slow learners, though later chapters will discuss the different needs which exist within the population.

How many slow learners?

In order to estimate the number of slow learners in the school population it is necessary to establish a standard by which the slow learners may be defined. To do this, educationists have made use of concepts developed by Burt (1937). Burt introduced the term 'educational age' related to scores on standardized tests of attainment in school subjects. On such tests a group of ten-year-old pupils have an average educational age of 10, ranging from 9·5 to 10·5: nine-year-old pupils range from 8·5 to 9·5 with an average educational age of 9 years. Burt also defined backward pupils as those who, in the middle of their school careers, are unable to do the work of the class next below that which is normal for their age (ibid., pp. 77-8). Thus, on standardized attainment tests, a backward ten-year-old pupil would have an educational age below 8·5 years: a definition adopted by the Ministry of Education (1937, pp. 9-12). Such a criterion has been referred to as a 'difference score' (P. Williams, 1970). A modification of this approach took the form of a 'percentage difference', regarding as backward pupils with 'educational ages' 20 per cent or more below their chronological ages (Ministry of Education, 1946); the advantage claimed for this procedure being that it facilitated the comparison of the incidence of backwardness in different age-groups. Using this criterion a backward pupil would have an educational age less than 80 per cent of his chronological age. Subsequently tests were developed which made use of 'deviation quotients' or 'standardized scores'. In such tests scores are 'normally' distributed around a mean score of 100 with a standard deviation of 15 points. Some 68 per cent of children tested on these standardized attainment tests will score between 85 and 115 points, these scores being regarded as marking off the 'normal limits' of the tests (S. Jackson, 1968, pp. 31-8; Vernon, 1960, pp. 105-11). On this criterion backward pupils will have 'deviation quotients' or 'standardized scores' of 85 or below.

In the above discussion the term 'backward pupil' has been used in order to remain consistent with the usage of the authors quoted in the references upon which the discussion is based. A standard has been outlined which marks out the population of slow learners as we defined them. It was also necessary to establish the standard before going on to discuss the results of surveys which have used the different methods of assessing educational retardation, as well as using the additional criterion of intelligence test scores. Intelligence test scores, for the purpose of this discussion, may be regarded as further examples of the 'deviation quotients' or 'standardized scores' discussed above: a 'dull' or 'intellectually retarded' pupil being defined by an intelligence test score of 85 or below.

One of the difficulties in attempting to estimate the incidence of backwardness in the schools is the lack of figures based upon any national survey. The surveys assembled below have been conducted at different times and in different areas; they have used tests differing in standardization and norms; they have defined backwardness by slightly different criteria; and there are variations in the number of subject tests used to arrive at the educational age or quotient. Nevertheless, in very broad terms, they do mark out the slow learner as described above. Burt (1937) estimated backward pupils to be between 10 per cent and 14 per cent of the school population, based on studies conducted from 1917 onward and mainly in London. Hill (1939) reported studies carried out in Southend-on-Sea which suggested that 10-15 per cent of secondary school pupils were backward to a degree which required more than the provision of education in a 'C' stream class. The Ministry of Education (1946) estimated that 10 per cent of the school population would need 'special educational treatment', a marked reduction of the 1937 figure of 18-19 per cent (Ministry of Education, 1937, pp. 9-13). A survey of the whole junior school population of Brighton (Hammond, 1948) indicated that at age ten and over, 15·1 per cent of boys and 10 per cent of girls had reading ages of below eight years. Schonell (1949) summarized a number of surveys and concluded that 2-3 per cent of the school population would have intelligence quotients (I.Q.) of between 55 and 70 whilst another 12-14 per cent would fall between 70 and 85 I.Q. According to Schonell's estimates slow learners would form 14-17 per cent of the school population. To some extent the progress made by pupils through the books of the popular primary reading schemes may be used as an estimate of their progress towards competent reading skill and, when pupils of the same age are considered, it is possible to estimate the numbers of pupils who are failing to make normal progress. Morris (1959, 1966) used this method with pupils in the schools of Kent during 1954. In her study it was considered that pupils who had not mastered Book 1 of their reading scheme by the age of seven were 'poor and non-readers': by this measure 19·2 per cent of the pupils were considered to be backward in reading. In 1957 Morris conducted another survey of Kent schools and on the same criterion found 14 per cent of the pupils to be non-readers or poor readers. Similarly, Hammond (1963) repeated her earlier study in Brighton during 1962, finding that amongst pupils of ten years of age or over, 10·5 per cent of the boys and 6·2 per cent of the girls had reading ages below eight years (see also Hammond, 1967). A substantial piece of work was the report of the First Child Development Study, 1958 Cohort (Pringle et al., 1966), which was based upon a study of 11,000 children who had reached the age of seven in 1965: the same pupils reported on in the Plowden Report (vol. 2, App. 10). Assessments in the study were based upon objective tests and teachers' estimates, with, for reading, progress on reading primers as described in relation to Morris above. The results of this study are summarized and tabulated:

Reading: On the Word Recognition Test 18 per cent were considered 'poor' readers (score 15 or below); on teachers' estimates 26 per cent were rated below average, including 3 per cent who were non-readers; for reading primers 9·8 per cent were on Book 1 or below.

Arithmetic: On the Problem Arithmetic Test 43 per cent could be considered 'poor' (score 4 or below); on teachers' estimates 36 per cent showed 'poor facility ... or ... little if any ability'.

Oral ability: Assessed only on teachers' ratings, 21 per cent were below average or markedly poor in conversation.

Awareness of the world around: Assessed only on teachers' estimates, 29 per cent were considered 'rather limited [in] knowledge ... or ... largely ignorant of the world around'.

Creativity: Assessed only on teachers' estimates, 33 per cent showed 'little originality in any ... work'.

Special educational help in ordinary school: 'Apart from anything which the class teacher may do', 5 per cent of the pupils were receiving special help. Of those not receiving help, according to head teachers, 8 per cent would benefit from help. Thus at least 13 per cent of the sample appear to need special teaching within the ordinary school.

Special educational treatment in the future: An examination of head teachers' responses indicated that 7 per cent of the pupils would require 'some form of special schooling or other special educational help within the next two years'. There is some ambiguity about the replies here when compared with the previous section. The authors consider that this reflects (a) the view of heads that some pupils would respond successfully to the help they were receiving, and (b) that the terminology, 'benefit from' (special help) in the previous section contrasted with 'need' (special educational treatment) in the present, has influenced replies. Nevertheless the report considers the figure of 7 per cent to be a minimum. (The report should be consulted for a full discussion of this problem.)

The report suggests that there is need to re-examine

9

official figures of the number of pupils likely to require special education in ordinary schools and particularly in the infant schools. It also offers significant evidence of a higher percentage of boys than girls in need of special educational provision. In 1968 the Inner London Education Authority (ILEA, 1969) conducted a survey of all eight-year-old pupils in Inner London schools, using a reading comprehension test standardized by the National Foundation for Educational Research on a nation-wide sample of 3,000 children. A standardized score on the test of 80 or below was used to define 'poor' readers, a category in which 17 per cent of the pupils were placed. This percentage is higher than in the standardization sample, where only 8·6 per cent were 'poor' readers. The report discusses the special circumstances which may account for the higher percentage of 'poor' readers in London, circumstances that are to some extent replicated in other cities or industrial conurbations which might well reflect the trend of London rather than the country-wide average. Meanwhile, in Dunbartonshire, Clark (1970) tested 1,544 children on the Schonell Graded Word Reading Test using a reading quotient of 85 or below to identify backward readers. She found that 15·3 per cent of the seven-year-old pupils were backward – 18 per cent of the boys and 12·5 per cent of the girls – with retesting at eight years old showing that over half of these were still backward and required help with basic reading. During 1970-1 Start and Wells (1972) tested a sample of 7,150 pupils in 300 schools. They found 8-9 per cent of eleven-year-olds with reading ages below seven years; 10 per cent of fifteen-year-olds with reading ages below eleven years; 0·4 per cent of the total sample illiterate (reading age below seven years) and 15·1 per cent semi-literate (reading age below nine years).

During 1967-8 members of H.M. Inspectorate carried out a survey of slow learners in secondary schools, the report of which was not published until December 1971 (DES, 1971). Questionnaires were completed by 28 comprehensive schools and 128 secondary modern schools covering a population of 91,527 pupils: each school was also visited by members of the Inspectorate. The sample represented 7·6 per cent of comprehensive schools and 5·8 per cent of modern schools spread over nine counties and eleven county boroughs, a total of twenty LEAS. It is considered as providing a 'reasonably reliable picture' of the situation in England.

In the opinion of the headteachers, largely confirmed by the HMIS, 12,807 pupils, almost exactly 14 per cent of the schools' population, required some form of special education, mainly as slow learners. Of these slow learners, 6,892 were receiving special education in their present school, about 54 per cent of those considered to require it. The headteachers also indicated that 682 pupils had difficulties severe enough to merit education in a special school, a sub-group which includes 5·4 per cent of the slow learners or 0·75 per cent of the total survey population. Examination of the estimates of slow learners showed that over one-third of the schools placed their estimate between 11 per cent and 20 per cent, but the range was wide with one school in seven placing the estimate above 20 per cent and the highest estimate reaching 60 per cent, a figure noted as exceptional but not unrealistic by the visiting inspectors.

What, then, is the outcome of these attempts to determine the proportion of slow learners in the schools? Before attempting to summarize, certain comments are required. The first year of the junior school is not the best base from which to estimate the future incidence of backwardness, particularly in reading. At that point many intellectually dull or immature pupils are not at the stage of readiness for formal reading instruction, but given reasonable conditions together with adequate and appropriate teaching they begin to master the skill during the year. As a result estimates made too early tend to overestimate the size of the problem, a situation which has been remarked upon by many remedial teachers as a result of their experience. Clark (1970) seems to lend support to this view and similar experience may have influenced the reduced estimate of future as against current need for special treatment reflected in the opinions of headmasters in responding to the Child Development Study Inquiry (Pringle et al., 1966). On the other hand, it has been suggested, on the basis of firm data, that pupils backward in reading at eight plus usually fail to make good their deficiency by the end of their school life (Morris, 1966), which certainly creates pressures for the early identification of the slow learners. However – to survey the surveys. The studies reported above show the range of estimates to be from 8 per cent to 24 per cent, and 13 per cent might reasonably reflect the general trend of the studies. Slow learners as 13 per cent of the schools' population? How does such an estimate stand in relation to the question as to whether standards in our schools are rising?

Are slow learners decreasing?

There is some evidence for the view that standards in schools have been improving during the period covered by the discussion of the previous section. Between 1951 and 1957 Wiseman (1964) found that in Manchester schools reading achievement increased, extreme backwardness amongst fourteen-year-olds falling from 4 to 2·4 per cent. Hammond (1967), reported that backwardness in reading amongst boys fell by 4·6 per cent and amongst girls by 3·8 per cent. Morris (1966) showed that reading standards in Kent rose between 1954 and 1957 and backwardness was reduced from 19 to 14 per cent. Surveys conducted between 1948 and 1964 by the Department of Education and Science (1967b) showed a continuing increase in reading standards with a reduction in the percentage of backward readers. The mean scores for pupils of eleven years on successive surveys were: 1948 – 11·6; 1952 – 12·4; 1956 – 13·3; 1964 – 15·0. This progress represents an increase in reading age of seventeen months or an increase in the pace of learning of 24 per cent. Further, a standardized score of 80 is represented by a percentile score of 10. In 1948 the tenth percentile score was 3·9 and 5 per cent of pupils were scoring two points or lower; by 1964 the tenth percentile score had risen to 7·5 and hardly any pupils fell below two points (DES, 1967a, vol. 2, p. 261). For fifteen-year-olds similar improvements had taken place. Mean scores for successive surveys were: 1948 – 18·0; 1952 – 18·4; 1956 – 18·9; 1961 – 21·3. Between 1948 and 1961 the rise in score represents a rise in reading age of twenty-three months or an increase in learning pace of 32 per cent (DES, 1963, p. 185). These improved standards are very encouraging to teachers but optimism should be moderated by caution. As Reid (1970) points out, the 10 per cent of eleven-year-olds who scored less than 7 in 1964 represent a group of near-illiterate pupils leaving the primary schools and the 1948 base-line itself may have represented a decline from 1938 standards as a result of the war years with the attendant disruption in the schools. Gulliford (1969, p. 9) recognized the 'continuing hard core of backwardness in schools', whilst, according to P. Williams (1970, p. 475), 'in spite of the great improvements in educational standards, the incidence of slow learners needing some form of special help still seems to lie between 10 per cent and 20 per cent'. Start and Wells (1972) used tests which allowed them to relate their reading survey of 1970-1 to the results of the surveys noted above which showed reading standards steadily increasing between 1948 and 1964 (DES, 1967b). They showed that in 1971 the reading standard of bright eleven-year-olds was three months of reading age below that of 1964 whilst the standard for the weaker 10 per cent had fallen by three and a half months, the overall standards having regressed to the levels of 1960. For fifteen-year-olds the results were similar, the survey showing that the improvement in reading standards between 1948 and 1961 had stopped between 1961 and 1971. The authors note certain limitations in their work as the proportion of non-participating schools was high, many pupils were absent from testing and the tests had become somewhat out-dated, but they hold that the inference of a halt in the improvement of reading standards in the last decade remains valid.

The evidence points to a clear conclusion. Measured by reading ability, there was a steady decline in the number of backward pupils and an increase in reading standards until the mid-1960s, though a hard core of backwardness persisted in the schools. The improvement now appears to be halted and there may be danger of an increase in the hard-core problem.

The number of slow learners in ordinary schools

There are no official returns from which the number of slow learners can be reckoned and it is necessary to estimate this figure. In January 1973 there were 8,081,688 pupils in the schools between ages 5 and 16 of whom 81,816 were in special schools for educationally subnormal pupils, whilst a further 11,288 pupils were awaiting admission to such schools (DES, 1973). At 13 per cent of the schools population, slow learners number 1,050,608. Deducting the number of pupils in ESN schools gives the total of slow learners in ordinary schools as 968,792 and even if those awaiting admission to ESN schools were provided for, the ordinary schools would still be faced with the need to provide an appropriate education for 957,504 slow learning pupils. It must be stressed that this is a *conservative* estimate which includes only those pupils whose education will require modification of the school curriculum, school organization, or both.

A responsibility of the ordinary school

The question often arises as to whether provision for slow learners should be through the provision of more special schools or through the expansion of facilities within the ordinary schools. It is interesting to examine some *facts* which bear on this question. In the last decade provision of special school places has averaged just over 2,100 per year; at ten times this annual rate of expansion it would be fifty years before places were provided for the number of slow learners at present in the schools. Thus, even if it were educationally desirable, to provide for slow learners exclusively in special schools is not a practicable proposition and the simple truth to be faced is that if slow learners are to have an education specially suited to their needs, then for 85 per cent of them that education will have to be provided within the ordinary schools.

This is not an argument against the provision of an adequate number of special schools. In any comprehensive attempt to meet the needs of slow learners, the provision of special school places for the 1-2 per cent of pupils with most serious learning difficulties will be necessary, but, numerically, this is the smaller part of the problem. The remaining, larger part of the problem can only be resolved by the provision of adequate facilities for slow learners within the ordinary schools. *That is why the education of slow-learning pupils is, and must remain, a responsibility to be accepted within the ordinary schools.* Neither is there any question of such provision being in any way 'second best'; indeed, for the majority of slow learners, the ordinary school is the *best* place in which to meet their educational needs. Once this is accepted it becomes possible to define the real problem. And that problem is fourfold for it requires: (1) the provision of an adequate number of special schools properly located in relation to the population of slow learners and complementing facilities within the ordinary schools; (2) the development within both types of schools of efficient programmes relevant to the needs of the slow learners for whom they are responsible; (3) the development of co-operation between the schools so that the system may attain flexibility in meeting the needs of slow learners; and (4) the development of techniques of *educational* assessment which will continually ensure that slow learners are in the schools best fitted to meet their educational needs.

Difficulties in the current situation.

A number of aspects of the current situation in the education of slow learners have been examined in the literature. Variety in provision has been discussed by S. Jackson (1966), Segal (1967) and Furneaux (1969); there has been comparative evaluation of the ordinary school and special school (Younghusband *et al.*, 1970, pp. 219-27; Gulliford, 1969, pp. 93-101; 1971, pp. 1-23 and 68-80; Green, 1969; Ascher, 1970); and there has been discussion of the means of providing for slow learners in the ordinary school (DES, 1963, 1964, 1967a, 1971, 1972; Cleugh, 1968; Gulliford, 1971, pp. 71-4). What this literature fails to mark out clearly is the fortuitous and hazardous nature of the circumstances which surround the education of the slow learners in the ordinary school. Their education is fortuitous because it seems to depend more upon the willingness of individual teachers or the availability of accommodation than upon rational and continuous planning by education authorities (Sampson, 1969, pp. 3-8 and 61-5; Sampson and Pumphrey, 1970, pp. 102-11; Cuthbert, 1971, pp. 34-6). This is an unfortunate circumstance when related to the wide local variations in the incidence of slow learners in the school population; the connection between the variation and the social backgrounds of the pupils; and the relationship between language codes and learning. These conditions require continuous identification of slow learners if their educational needs are to be planned for on a rational basis, and it is the absence throughout the system of such organized attempts to locate the problem which contributes most to the fortuitous situation of the slow learners. But this fortuitous education of the slow learner is also hazardous. It is hazardous because even where good conditions are established they are unlikely to persist throughout the school life of the pupil. In the short term, classes for slow learners are often the first to be disrupted by the reallocation of their teachers to other duties whenever staff shortages create crisis in the school. In the long term, good work frequently vanishes without trace should the teacher responsible for it move on to another school. Both these conditions reflect the low status which is accorded to work with slow learners in the ordinary schools as well as the absence of any clear career structure for teachers in this area of education (Brennan, 1971).

Summary

Slow learners are defined as pupils who do not have above average intellectual ability or severe intellectual retardation or any other primary handicap but who are unable to cope with school work considered normal for their age-group; they communicate using speech and they relate to others in a normal manner though they may exhibit some immaturity or insecurity arising from their experience of failure. It is estimated that such pupils form 13 per cent of the school population, 1,050,608 pupils, of whom 968,792 are at present in the ordinary schools. In the past twenty-five years there has been steady improvement in the extent and quality of educational provision for slow learners and some evidence of improvement in their attainments, though there is now evidence that the improvement may have been halted. Further improvement is seen as depending upon the development of a more rational and continuously planned approach to the provision of facilities for slow learners, mainly within the ordinary schools, though in co-operation with special schools and related to the identification of slow learners in the local school population. To be fully effective, such an approach must improve the status which is accorded to work with slow learners in the ordinary schools and should create a clear career structure for the teachers involved in it.

2 Some characteristics of slow learners

The study of the characteristics of slow learners should safe-guard the teacher from the dangers created by general definitions which were noted in chapter 1. Such study is, however, complicated by the absence of agreed definitions in this area of education. More than in other areas, the education of the slow learner is partly the province of psychologists and doctors as well as teachers. Doctors, psychologists and teachers view this section of the school population from different points and the categories they develop are designed to serve different purposes; it is not surprising, therefore, to find that the labels attached to the categories also differ. Two other circumstances also add to the confusion. Much of the literature originates in the USA and reflects the basic differences between the educational system of that country and the educational system in Britain. Furthermore, many of the categorizations, though important, relate to problems, often clinical in nature, which rarely operate in relation to the population of slow learners as defined in chapter 1 of this book (Brison, 1967).

In this chapter an attempt will be made to examine the characteristics of slow learners and the examination will be confined to characteristics which affect their education. This must not be taken to imply that the categories developed for other purposes are without value; it is merely that they may be less important in the general question of how the slow learner should be educated and the more specific question of the methods which should be used to teach him.

Burt (1937) classified characteristics of his backward pupils as: inherited conditions; environmental conditions relating to (a) school and (b) home; physical conditions, either (a) developmental or (b) pathological; and psychological conditions of (a) intellect and (b) temperament. He refined the above conditions to sixteen sub-groups and concluded that in the typical backward pupil 'not one cause, but several, are at work'. This is the concept of 'multiplicity of causation' which is even more fully appreciated at the present time. Similar to these classifications are those proposed by Robinson and Robinson (1965) and of special note is their section on psychological damage, dealing with: inadequate early care (institutionalization, sensory deprivation, rejection, indifferent maternal care), subnormal parents, family size, education, social class, ethnic or racial group, and interpsychic variables (achievement motivation, anxiety). P. Williams (1970) has commented on the Robinson scheme and indicated the need for more adequate assessment of educational factors, sensory stimulation and emotional conditions (pp. 495-8). Schonell (1942) developed and modified the scheme proposed by Burt in classifying the sources of individual differences in children. His scheme included: intellectual characteristics (general intelligence, specific mental abilities, level of school attainments), emotional tendencies (instinctive and emotional impulses, interests and complexes), physical conditions (constitution, specific physical advantages or defects, general physical condition), and environmental influences (within school, in society, at home). There are some redundancies in Schonell's scheme, e.g. physical defect included twice, and, like Burt, he is far from clear in discussing the concepts of acquired or innate differences, even going so far as to consider 'partly inborn' characteristics (pp. 17-49). These summaries have been placed together to enable the reader to note the emphasis on intelligence and genetic factors in the schemes of Burt and Schonell and to contrast this with the typical American study of the Robinsons, who do not stress the inherited nature of intelligence but do emphasize environmental factors. To some extent these are general differences in the USA and British positions, but they do also reflect change in time and new knowledge influencing concepts of the roles of environment and inheritance in the development of human abilities and attainments.

Dullness, backwardness and retardation

The concepts of dullness, backwardness and retardation follow from the work of Schonell (1942). *Dullness* was held to be characterized by intellectual deficiency as indicated by the results of intelligence tests; it was held to be almost invariably accompanied by general backwardness. *Backwardness* was represented as scholastic deficiency indicated by a failure to perform on standardized tests of attainment at a level commensurate with chronological age; such backwardness might be *general*, over all subject areas, or *specific* to certain subject areas. It was also held that both general or specific backwardness might be either *remediable* or *irremediable*. *Retardation* was defined as a condition of unrealized intellectual ability represented by scores on scholastic tests at a level below the scores on intelligence tests, in other words, by a failure to perform on scholastic tests at a level consistent with mental age. Such retardation might exist in association with high, average or low intellectual ability; it could be general or specific in nature. Schonell regarded retardation as 'an assessment from an individual standpoint of educational level in relation to intellectual capacity'. Backwardness he regarded as 'an assessment from a group standpoint of educational level in relation to chronological age capacity' (ibid., p. 66). From this work of Schonell's there developed the concept of the 'achievement quotient' using mental age and attainment age obtained from standardized tests in the formula:

$$\frac{\text{Attainment age}}{\text{Mental age}} \times 100 = \text{Achievement quotient}$$

From these related concepts were derived certain alleged characteristics of slow-learning pupils. Such pupils could be:

(a) dull and backward:
  chronological age 10; mental age 8.
  attainment age 8; achievement quotient 100.
(b) dull, backward and retarded:
  chronological age 10; mental age 8.
  attainment age 6; achievement quotient 75.
(c) backward and retarded:
  chronological age 10; mental age 10.
  attainment age 8; achievement quotient 80.
(d) retarded:
  chronological age 10; mental age 12.
  attainment age 10; achievement quotient 83.

Though Schonell himself made reservations about the use of general ability as the sole determinant of school attainment (ibid., p. 74n.), his followers made the above scheme almost the sole approach to the classification of slow learners for many years. Collins (1961) criticized the concepts of 'backwardness' and 'retardation'. A. A. Williams (1970) summarizes the objections based upon difficulties in defining intelligence, the influence upon intelligence of environmental variables and cultural background, low correlations between non-verbal intelligence tests and reading test scores and miscellaneous variations in test construction and interpretation (pp. 16-18). P. Williams (1970) quotes the work of Phillips (1961) and shows how he indicated an improved rationale for the interpretation of retardation which removed some of the objections by Collins (1961). A similar approach was used by Savage and O'Connor (1966) to calculate regression equations which would provide greater precision in the assessment of retardation (P. Williams, 1970, pp. 481-3; Savage, 1968, pp. 51-3).

Duncan (1942), in describing the characteristics of backward children, introduced the concept of *concrete* intelligence suggested by Alexander (1935). Duncan held that the assessment of the intelligence of backward children through the use of verbal intelligence tests seriously underrated the level of their general intelligence, which was more accurately sampled by the use of performance tests requiring them to

operate in concrete, practical situations. To support this contention he quoted the results from his own school in Hamp-
shire, England as:

Stanford Revision (Verbal) Test – IQ range 54-76, mean 66.
Alexander Test (Performance) – IQ range 67-119, mean 96.

Duncan claimed that this characteristic could be made the
starting point for teaching which could improve the attainments and problem-solving powers of slow-learning pupils.
Subsequent commentators have suggested that Duncan
generalized too freely from the population of his *rural* school
to that of backward children in general; that he did not allow
sufficiently for emotional maladjustment or poor language
experience; and that his claim for generalization of results
from concrete thinking to abstract thinking remains
unproven (Kirk and Johnson, 1951; Tansley and Gulliford,
1960). However that may be, it should be noted that Duncan
did not differ from Burt and Schonell in his use of the concepts of dullness, backwardness and retardation, or in his
use of the achievement quotient; he merely differed in the
way *general* ability should be measured in arriving at the
mental age of the pupil.

The concepts of dullness, backwardness, retardation, the
achievement quotient and the associated concept of learning
difficulties being *remediable* or *irremediable*, together with
the idea of slow learners being more efficient in *concrete*
learning situations, all derive from the work of Burt, Schonell
and Duncan which dominated the approach to the education
of such pupils in the 1940s and 1950s. What is the status
of these concepts today?

Since 1960 a variety of new ideas have challenged the older
concepts. The powerful case against a predetermined and
fixed level of intelligence has been summarized by Hunt
(1961, 1967); the relationship between environmental variables, intelligence and attainment has been documented by
Wiseman (1964), Douglas (1964, 1968), Pringle *et al.* (1966)
and Ravenette (1970); while Phillips (1961), Fransella and
Grever (1966) and Savage and O'Connor (1966) have shown
that the concept of the achievement quotient must be exten-

sively revised if it is to continue as a basis for population surveys or the assessment of individual pupils. The work of Piaget (Beard, 1969; Flavell, 1963) has shown how the developmental lag in the thinking of slow-learning pupils may result in a later and longer period at the level of *concrete operations* and thus explain their greater efficiency in dealing with situations providing sensory input, a better explanation for Duncan's findings than that which he proposed. These converging ideas suggest that genetic inheritance and environmental circumstances are far too interactive to be separated for practical purposes of education. In turn, this means that the concepts of dullness, backwardness and retardation cannot be assessed as *remediable* or *irremediable* on the sole criterion of standardized testing and, in these circumstances, the idea of under- or over-achievement has little meaning in relation to individual pupils. If these concepts are to retain any value they must increasingly be based upon a diagnosis of learning difficulties derived from careful observation of the pupil's response in learning situations over a period of time. This is *educational* diagnosis in the classroom rather than *psychological* diagnosis in the clinic.

Other educational characteristics

Making use of their own creative educational experience, Tansley and Gulliford (1960) used an operational approach to place slow-learning pupils into three categories related to their educational needs (pp. 6-14, 41-5).

1   Children with retardation in mental development and additional handicaps such as physical deficiency, ill-health, limited language experience and emotional disturbance. The problems of these children require education in special schools or in special classes in the ordinary schools with aims and methods similar to special schools.

2   Children whose ability is less limited but who have more difficulty in learning than normal pupils due to school absence, unfortunate personal circumstances or inadequate environmental circumstances. Failure to recognize the needs

of this group was suggested as an additional condition contributing to their difficulties. It was suggested that groups 1 and 2 could not be simply differentiated but that most of the latter group could be educated in ordinary schools either in special classes or by other methods.

3 Children not manifestly limited in intelligence but still at the beginning stages of reading and writing. Such children were held to reveal their higher ability by average attainment in other, practical subjects, or by richness of oral expression or variety of interests. Emotional maladjustment or perceptual difficulty of a specific nature were suggested as contributing to failure in this group. The provision of special or remedial teaching (presumably within the ordinary school) was to form the educational provision for this group.

In addition to these broad characteristics, Tansley and Gulliford also summarized other features associated with slow learners. In intellectual development they stress the limitation to Piaget's *concrete* stage (as noted above) and relate this to functional weakness in attention, perception and memory. They also note the general emotional immaturity of slow learners which they hold to be influenced by the limited time perspectives induced through intellectual limitations; the effect of educational and social failure; the action of delayed or uneven emotional growth; and possible inadequacies in the home. Physical defects associated with slow learners they placed into three groups; those where delayed physical development coincided with and contributed to delays in other areas of growth; those where average or better physical development outpaced mental development, thus creating a different set of problems; and those where capacity to learn is reduced by the continuous, cumulative effect of minor illness, ailment or defect (ibid., pp. 33-72). Relying heavily upon the work of Strauss and Lehtinen (1947) they describe the so-called 'brain-injured' child as showing muscular incoordination, perceptual inaccuracy, conceptual disorders, perseveration of behaviour patterns and hyperactivity based upon restlessness, distractability and inability to delay satisfaction (1960, pp. 81-6).

Slow Learners At School (DES, 1964) provided an excellent summary of the characteristics of slow learners. Of particular interest is the statement on the relative importance of heredity and environment (p. 7):

> Though few people would now dispute that heredity plays an important part in determining the upper limits of intellectual growth, research which has taken place in the last fifteen or twenty years and has greatly increased our knowledge of the intellectual and temperamental characteristics of backward children leads us to believe that the various influences combining to form the child's environment exercise a wider and more potent effect on his development than had once been assumed. The psychological and material conditions in which a child grows up play a very vital part in determining the equipment he brings to learning. Only when environmental conditions are ideal will a child's hereditary endowment determine the upper limit of his development.

The work lists five important conditions associated with learning difficulties: the importance of mother-love for *intellectual* as well as emotional development; the maturation of the central nervous system and the relation of its growth to critical periods in learning; the effect of language retardation on the child's ability to utilize learning situations in school; the influence of sensory defect on learning ability; and the insidious effect of unsatisfactory school conditions upon the child's learning. The characteristics of slow learners are classified into those observable in the first year in school and others which may be observed later. Early signs are listed as: lack of interest in toys or pictures; delayed or retarded language or vocabulary development; inability to join in play; and behaviour which disturbs the work of other children. The later signs of difficulty include: slowness in learning to read; difficulty in concept formation; difficulty in generalizing from learning; limited ability to generalize from experience, which may itself be restricted; the presence of delayed or distorted emotional development which may be due to experience of continued failure or lack of success (pp. 7-17).

Gulliford (1969, 1971) defined four levels of backwardness largely on the basis of the kind of specialized help needed and the intellectual level indicated by the results of intelligence tests as:

Severely subnormal showing severe intellectual limitation, lack of capacity for academic school work and a need for programmes promoting personal and social development usually provided in schools for severely mentally handicapped children.

Educationally subnormal who for 'reason of limited ability or other conditions resulting in educational retardation require some specialized form of education wholly or partly in substitution for the education normally given in ordinary schools'. This is the official definition of ESN pupils. Gulliford suggests that about 1 per cent of the school population is provided for in special schools or classes for ESN children: in fact, this percentage is best regarded as the number provided for in *special schools as there are no accurate national figures to indicate the extent of provision in properly organized special classes*. He does, however, indicate that the population of ESN pupils is much larger than the number of pupils placed in the special schools or classes.

Slow learners who require special consideration in terms of the organization, curriculum and method of their education. These pupils are largely in ordinary schools distributed widely and unevenly but estimated at about 15 per cent of the school population.

Retarded children of average or good intelligence who are failing in all or some aspects of their school work, the assumption being that special remedial teaching may bring them to a level of attainment more commensurate with their manifest abilities.

Gulliford stresses the multiplicity of factors causing backwardness and particularly notes the high percentage of backward pupils with IQs above 70 as well as the pupils from backgrounds of high social status, in this he relies heavily upon the work of Chazan (1964) and he frames the inference that the high-social-status group amongst backward pupils may result from individuals with severe learning difficulties which are neurological (organic) in origin.

Reorganizing the categories of backward pupils according to the main causative factor, Gulliford identifies five groups:

Pupils with limited intelligence. These represent two populations: a sub-group which may be made up of those individuals who represent the lower part of the curve of normal distribution of intellectual ability; and a further sub-group whose low functional level is the result of defects of the central or peripheral nervous system – the so-called neurological or organic defects.

Culturally and/or socially disadvantaged pupils. These are pupils in whom ability and attainment suffer from inadequate sensory stimulation in early life, allied to inadequate language background and general absence of continuing rich and varied experience.

Pupils with personality difficulties or maladjustment. Many of the conditions resulting in cultural or social deprivation also penalize children in relation to normal emotional development. Such conditions often make relationships and communication difficult for the pupil and thus inhibit or distort his response to learning situations presented in school.

Pupils with specific learning difficulties. In these pupils there are functional difficulties affecting attention, perception, sensory integration, physical co-ordination, due either to delays or malfunctions in the neural systems which support the functions. These specific difficulties may be present at any level of ability and exhibit their presence through learning failure.

Children with Handicaps. These are children with milder sensory or physical handicaps of sight, hearing or motor ability, some of whom are to be found in the ordinary schools.

Naturally all these factors may overlap in some pupils and 'pure' cases are a theoretical rather than a real occurrence, but often a major factor can be identified. Perhaps the categories are best regarded as defining areas in which may reside the 'needs' of individual slow learners.

A. A. Williams (1970) uses a scheme of classification similar to that outlined by Gulliford. He continues, however, to make use of the term 'backward' in the sense used in our discussion of the achievement quotient. He quotes more extensively from Chazan (1964) in outlining the characteristics of socially deprived children as showing: inadequacies in symbolization and language; deficiencies in visual and auditory perception; short attention span; inability to delay gratification; poor self concepts and feelings of inferiority; low motivation in school learning; school withdrawal; and general behaviour problems. He also makes more direct use of the term 'brain injury' as a characteristic of some slow learners. In this he relies on Strauss and Lehtinen (1947) and Kirk and Johnson (1951) in summarizing the features of this syndrome as: perceptual disorders in confusion of background and foreground or difficulty in part/whole discrimination; disorders of concepts and thought shown in unusual and bizarre approaches to learning or problem solving; perseveration, or the persistent repetition of motor, behavioural or language sequences once started, particularly in association with abnormal fixation of interest; and behaviour disorder of a hyperactive or distractible nature. This is generally the pattern often referred to in the literature as the 'Strauss syndrome' or 'minimal cerebral dysfunction' and these terms themselves overlap with the term 'organic'. It should be noted that though the syndrome described may be useful in discussing the needs of certain slow learners, the whole situation is confused by multiplicity of terminology and subtle differences in definition. Central to the confusion is the use of a neurological label for an educational–behavioural syndrome. In an attempt to avoid confusion the term 'learning disabilities' is coming into use, particularly at the level represented by our definition of the slow learner (Johnson and Myklebust, 1967; Tarnopol, 1969). What is quite certain, however, is that terms which carry a neurological connotation should never be used in relation to children merely upon the evidence of classroom observation by teachers.

Gulliford (1971) is also critical of the use of the term

'brain-injured' in education. Using the work of Birch (1964), Gulliford notes that not all children exhibiting the 'Strauss syndrome' can be shown to be neurologically damaged, whilst others who appear to be so damaged do not exhibit the syndrome! (pp. 67-8). Both the term and the *stereotype* of the 'brain-injured child' should be avoided by psychologists and teachers who should 'observe and assess disorders and severe developmental lags in perception, perceptual-motor, thinking and language skills so that teaching can be prescribed to remedy the weakness' (p. 68). However, Gulliford does suggest that the teacher's awareness that there may be an organic basis for the above difficulties can act as a safeguard against a too easy assumption that emotional factors or inadequate teaching are their primary causes.

In chapter 1 (p. 5) it was observed that there was general dissatisfaction with the term 'educationally subnormal' and that the objections were not completely met by the substitution of the term 'slow-learning pupil'. In *Living With Handicap* (Younghusband, *et al.*, 1970) an attempt has been made to organize handicaps into groups which have a more direct relationship to educational needs (pp. 204-19). Of the ten groups proposed four are directly related to slow learners as defined in this study. The four groups are: *intellectual handicap, severe environmental handicap, specific learning disorder* and *emotional handicap*. This relationship becomes clearer when it is noted that by proposing the categories of *severe personality disorder* and *severe multi-handicap* Younghusband removes from the above four groups those children whose learning difficulties constitute a secondary condition following from a severe primary handicap. Indeed, the four related groups represent rearrangements of the characteristics of intellectual retardation, organic or neurological impairment, social or cultural disadvantage and personality difficulty or maladjustment indicated in the work surveyed above. In contrast with the earlier work of Burt (1937), Schonell (1942) and Duncan (1942), the more recent trend is to relate the characteristics of slow learners to their life situations and experience, and to group them in ways which, whilst they certainly indicate possible causation, are more important in directing attention to the *needs* of children as the starting-points for educational provision.

Difficulties associated with slow learners

In addition to the major characteristics discussed above, other difficulties appear in association with slow learners, which, though they may not be the most important determinants of their learning failures, do contribute, often cumulatively, to the complex problems which they pose in the classroom. Two recent surveys illustrate these difficulties.

In the Isle of Wight survey (Rutter, 1966; Rutter *et al.*, 1970) 86 pupils aged 9-10 years, average IQ 94, and all at least 28 months retarded in reading were compared with a control group of 144 normal pupils. The backward group showed a higher degree of the following 'neurological' characteristics: less than perfect right–left orientation, 61·6 per cent; abnormal clumsiness, 8·1 per cent; and difficulty with constructional tasks, 7·0 per cent. In language and speech characteristics the backward exceeded the controls on the following: single word only after two years, 10·5 per cent; three-word phrase only after three years, 11·0 per cent; speech less complex than normal, 15·1 per cent; articulation defect, 14·0 per cent; parent or sibling with no speech after $2\frac{1}{2}$ years, 10·1 per cent; parent or sibling delayed in learning to read, 33·8 per cent. All the differences were statistically significant. Maladjustment in the groups was assessed by means of questionnaires completed by parents and, separately, by teachers. For anti-social type maladjustment from parental questionnaire the backward (12·2 per cent) exceeded the controls to a statistically significant degree. On teachers' questionnaires the backward exceeded the controls for both anti-social (23·3 per cent) and neurotic maladjustment (12·8 per cent), the difference being statistically significant.

The incidence of additional disabilities was also shown in the report *Slow Learners in Secondary Schools* (DES, 1971). In a population of 12,807 slow learners the following disabilities were recorded: defects of vision, 124; defects of hearing, 218; physical handicap, 222; epilepsy, 82; maladjustment, 483;

and 'other' disabilities, 603. In only a small number of cases did the disability merit the designation of 'handicapped pupil', though it was considered that many called for some measure of special care. One school of 600 pupils recorded the following disabilities: haemophilia (2), diabetes (1), otitis media (1), cerebral palsy (1), heart condition (6), gall bladder condition (1), bladder condition with incontinence (1), kidney condition (2), partial hearing (2), partial sight (2), osteo-myelitis (1), muscular disability (1), skin condition (1), asthma (14), stammer (2) and colour blindness (16). The survey concludes (p. 22):

> Though almost all of the pupils included in this survey had limited educational attainments ... not all were of limited intellectual capacity. Though there was, in many cases, good reason to doubt whether the figures for additional disabilities were either complete or accurate – and in many cases the yardstick was crude – it was obvious that many (perhaps the majority) of the pupils suffered from secondary disabilities.... Physical and sensory handicaps in varying degrees were frequent, maladjustment (a crude definition in this context) even commoner and adverse social conditions widespread ... it quickly became apparent that most of the pupils included in the category of slow learners had more than one difficulty to contend with.

Other research has also directed attention to difficulties which are commonly found in slow learners. Belmont and Birch (1964) showed that poor readers were significantly weak in integrating auditory and visual perception and in right–left orientation (1965). Ingram (1960, 1964, 1971) classified difficulties as visual–spatial, relating to writing and copying; sound–speech, representing confusion of sounds and speech; and association difficulties, generally a difficulty in relating speech and writing. Visual–motor difficulties relating to copy-ing, and auditory–motor difficulties relating to language or speech have been described by Wedell (1968). In another study De Hirsch *et al.* (1966) showed that in five-year-olds disorganized, impulsive overactivity, poor motor or visual–

31

motor abilities and poor expressive language are likely to indicate possible difficulties in learning to read. 'Clumsy' children, awkward in movement or posture and slow to develop manual–social skills have been described by Brenner *et al.* (1967), Gordon (1969), Morris and Whiting (1971). Using the Bristol Social Adjustment Guides, Stott (1963, 1966) identified an 'inconsequential', behavioural syndrome describing a very restless, careless and forgetful child, lacking in concentration and persistence. Subsequently Chazan (1968) found the syndrome in 17 per cent of children attending special classes for slow learners but only in 5·9 per cent of pupils in ESN special schools: in ordinary school classes only 1·8 per cent of pupils showed the 'inconsequential' syndrome. In a later study (Marston and Stott, 1970) the inconsequential syndrome was refined and related to a test of motor impairment. Inconsequential children showed a higher degree of motor impairment than the normal controls. Lovell and Gorton (1968) had used the same motor impairment test, together with tests of language, auditory–visual integration, sound–symbol association, spatial orientation and left–right discrimination in a study of backward and normal readers. On all these measures the backward group was inferior. Similar results have been shown for primary school pupils (Lovell, Shapton and Warren, 1964); in secondary pupils (Lovell, Gray and Oliver, 1964); and among senior pupils in ESN special schools (Lovell, White and Whitley, 1965).

These studies indicate clearly that the principle of 'multiplicity of causation' so well demonstrated by Burt (1937) still operates in relation to slow learners in school. But even more clearly they show the clustering of difficulties related to inadequacies of language, of motor control, of perceptual or visual–motor–perceptual function, of behaviour regulation and of concentration on current tasks. These difficulties are common to the descriptions of 'brain-injured children', 'clumsy' children and 'inconsequential' children. They certainly suggest that some learning difficulties could be associated with some dysfunction of the central nervous system (Lovell, 1966, pp. 127-47).

Wedell (1974), has recently surveyed the field of perceptual–

motor disabilities. He identifies and explains the functions contributing to sensory–motor development, relating disabilities to behavioural and educational difficulties. He also indicates that though extreme disabilities are clearly related to learning difficulties, the relationship is much less clear when the disabilities are at a mild level. In a good, critical discussion of available training programmes, Wedell suggests that they are more likely to improve general behavioural adequacies rather than specific skills such as reading. More important, he stresses the need to examine programmes in detail in an attempt to identify the specific elements or activities which contribute to any observed success.

These recent studies have extended and refined the conclusions reached by Burt. Amongst London children, he showed that, compared with their normal peers, the backward pupils came from poorer homes, larger families and overcrowded conditions; their fathers were likely to hold less skilled jobs and to be more often unemployed. The backward pupils were shorter and lighter than their normal peers; in temperament the group showed more deviants in the direction of *excitable* and also more in the direction of *repressed*; psycho-neurosis, anxiety states and neurasthenia were more frequent but not hysteria or minor neurotic symptoms. Not surprisingly, the backward group showed much poorer school attendance than their normal peers. Even counting physical conditions as one factor, the typical backward child showed three adverse factors influencing his school progress. The sociological and physical results from Burt's survey were substantially confirmed by the 1947 survey of Scottish school children (Scottish Council for Research in Education, 1953) and at the more intensive small-scale level by Croft (1951) and Brennan (1958). The latter studies also confirm Burt's findings of greater temperamental and emotional difficulties in the backward groups. In both studies the slow learners showed *non-social tendencies* and *social undervaluation* (Sanders, 1948) to a statistically significant degree when compared with normal children of the same age. Brennan (1958) also compared slow learners with their bright peers on the Bristol Social Adjustment Guide (Stott, 1963).

He showed that although more of the slow learners showed symptoms of maladjustment, the difference in degree of maladjustment between the two groups was not statistically significant. However, the slow learners did show significantly more unsettledness, whether judged by the number of boys showing symptoms or the total unsettledness in the groups. In a later study (Brennan, 1961), similar trends were shown for primary school pupils though the association between poor adjustment and low intelligence test score was statistically significant only at the nine- to ten-year-old level.

The interests of slow learners, both in and out of school, have not been widely studied, but the information is consistent. The lesson preferences of slow learners are not markedly different from those of their normal peers, though they are less stable and more directly influenced by relationships with teachers. Slow learners are less likely to be members of the school library but do not show differences in their choice of books. Out of school the slow learners are less likely to belong to a library, to attend church or belong to organized groups or gangs. Interests and hobbies do not differ markedly between the slow learners and their normal peers, though the latter do show better organization in their activities and better quality in their products. There is a tendency for normal pupils to be marginally more involved in activities which take them further from home and the slow learners have certainly travelled less and by less varied methods. In *number* of out-of-school activities there is little difference between slow learners and their normal peers, though the slow learners are more likely to go fishing and the normal children to go camping or play a musical instrument. Art galleries, exhibitions, theatres, seaports, and dental surgeries are more frequently visited by normal pupils, who have stayed more frequently in hotels or boarding-houses. On the other hand, cinemas are visited more frequently by slow learners. In their homes slow learners do slightly more work and receive pocket money in instalments rather than in the lump sum favoured for their peers, whilst, for the slow learner, discipline tends to rest on withdrawal of privilege in contrast to the explanatory methods favoured for normal children. The amount of radio listening or television viewing does not differ between slow learners and other children and there is little difference in programme choices (Croft, 1951; Brennan, 1958; J. A. Davies, 1959; Flemming *et al.*, 1960; Lovett, 1966; Howlett, 1968; T. G. Davies, 1969; Lawrence, 1969; National Association of Teachers of English, 1969).

Summary

Early attempts to classify the characteristics of slow learners were strongly influenced by concepts about the genetic basis of intelligence and the results of intelligence and attainment testing, though there was reference to the influence of personality and environmental variables. Later approaches place less stress on the 'global' nature of intelligence and more on the neurological systems and psychological functions which support learning and adaptive behaviour. These later approaches do not deny the genetic contribution to intelligence, but they place more stress upon the importance of interaction between the individual and his total environment.

The characteristics of slow learners are classified as: impairment or delay in intellectual development; impairment in perception, or in visual–motor–perceptual integration; associated social or cultural disadvantages; and personality difficulties or maladjustment. Usually more than one factor contributes to the learning failure of the slow-learning pupil.

3 The characteristics of slow learners reorganized

Previous chapters have surveyed accumulated knowledge about slow learners and indicated the conceptual frameworks which have been used to classify and discuss their characteristics. These conceptual frameworks have tended to be based upon the *causes* of learning difficulties and classification has placed considerable emphasis upon the results of intelligence and attainment testing. Recent formulations have begun to take account of the slow learner's educational needs but have not yet adequately tackled the problem of devising suitable curricula and learning experience for the different kinds of educational need found in slow learners. A further reformulation of the characteristics of slow learners, more directly related to the work of the teacher, is necessary if the 'individualization of treatment' advocated by Tansley and Gulliford (1960) is to become a reality in the schools. Such a reformulation or reorganization is attempted in this chapter.

Characteristics and educational needs

Any reorganization of characteristics related to educational needs, to be successful, must allow for a multiplicity of needs, not only between different pupils, but within the same pupil; and it must also allow for continual change in those needs as pupils mature and learn. To allow for this essential diversity and flexibility, characteristics are now related to three kinds of educational need: (1) the need for adaptive, developmental education; (2) the need for corrective education; (3) the need for remedial education.

Adaptive, developmental education

Adaptive, developmental education is the kind of education intended to meet the needs of slow learners who deviate markedly and permanently from their normal peers. The needs to be provided for may arise from intellectual, emotional or social characteristics, or from any combination of these, but a general characteristic of pupils requiring this kind of education is that learning is difficult over a wide range of activities, awareness is at a low level, motivation is at a low level and transient, interest is difficult to arouse and sustain, thought processes are restricted and verbal communication presents many problems. Standardized tests of ability and attainment provide useful pointers to pupils with these needs, though, for most pupils, skilled observation of responses in continuous teaching and learning situations will provide better clues to the child's basic educational needs.

The term *adaptive* is used to indicate that the pupil requires educational programmes which have been devised to meet his general, permanent learning needs. This is not a new concept, but in current usage adaptation of the curriculum is often thought of in a static manner, suggesting a once-and-for-all act on the part of the teacher or the school. Such thinking is educationally restrictive. It overlooks the fact that slow learners grow, mature and develop like other pupils, though at a slower, more variable rate. The use of the term *developmental* stresses the fact that though the needs are general and permanent they are not static and do alter and change as the pupil grows and matures. Consequently, adaptive, educational programmes must change, at least in order to keep pace with the pupil's actual development and, at best, in anticipation of that development in order to foster it efficiently.

It follows, therefore, that adaptive, developmental education has nothing 'short-term', 'corrective' or 'remedial' about it, if by such expressions is meant the 'putting right' of something as a result of which the pupil can subsequently be educated through curricular content and method appropriate for his normal peers. On the contrary, adaptive, developmental education must start from first principles and develop continuously throughout the education of the pupil. And the first principles are direct and simple. On one hand the teacher has knowledge of the pupil's overall ability; his patterns of strength and weakness in learning; his concept of himself; and the pattern and strength of his motivation. On the other hand the teacher is aware of the social and cultural situation of the pupil; the attitudes to school and learning which surround and influence him; his culturally determined perception of society and the place of the individual within it; the particular emphasis given to all this by the intimate ethos of the pupil's family and by the particular language patterns which mediate between the pupil and his environment. By relating his knowledge from these two sources and establishing priorities based upon intelligent anticipation of the 'life tasks' which will face the pupil, the teacher is able to determine the curriculum experiences which must be presented to the pupil. In organizing the experiences the teacher must be aware that the methods he uses not only establish communication with the pupil but also actively contribute in assisting the pupil to attain his curriculum goals. The detail of this is discussed in chapter 5, here it is sufficient to note that though the first principles are direct and simple, the interactions needed in the education of the pupil are exceedingly complex and require for success clearly formulated aims on the part of the teacher.

Provision throughout school life for the adaptive, developmental education of permanently handicapped pupils who need it is a *very real, important and continuing responsibility of the ordinary school.* This cannot be stressed too strongly, for it does require special provision in terms of both curriculum and school organization. At the time of writing, such provision is remarkable for its absence – particularly in secondary schools (National Association for Remedial Education, 1970; DES 1971).

Corrective education

Corrective education is the kind of education required to

meet needs which arise from specific limitations to learning. The specific limitations of pupils with such needs are largely in the basic areas of literacy and numeracy with the former closely related to the pupils' deficiencies in the use of language. As language itself is a major mediator between the individual and his environment, deficiency here is frequently associated with the pupil's immature perception of the world in which he lives and such pupils may also have difficulty in conceptualization. The characteristics associated with these needs and limitations are found in features of the pupil's environment or in his relationship to the environment. Inadequate stimulation in early life; poor language experience; the failure of parents in using the normal experience of childhood to stimulate curiosity and intellectual growth; the development of language *codes* or *registers* which differ in subtle ways from those used in schools; restricted access to books; inadequate or inappropriate early education – or absence of it; poor or irregular school attendance as a result of ill health or parental unconcern; frequent changes of school due to family migrations; unfortunate changes of teacher at periods critical for educational development; inadequate continuity of teaching within the school: these are the common characteristics which are associated with pupils who require corrective education. A complicating factor is that though these characteristics result in specific learning limitations for some pupils, for others they appear to have a generally depressing effect upon abilities as well as upon attainments. These latter pupils will require adaptive as well as corrective education. It is where the characteristics result in specific learning limitations not accompanied by general lowering of ability that successful corrective education may enable the pupil to pursue his education through the normal school curriculum.

Corrective education, then, is intended to enable the pupil to overcome limitations to learning which are the result of inadequate or missing experience, knowledge or skill by identifying the inadequacies or gaps and providing rich and varied learning experiences designed to compensate for them. Such education requires the school to intervene in the pupil's environment to enrich or restructure it, or to reshape the pupil's relation to it. In this intervention, traditional educational techniques can be very powerful, for they can, within broad limits, control, shape and enrich the sensory inputs which are the bedrock of the pupil's learning.

The provision of corrective education for those pupils who require it is also an important responsibility of the ordinary schools. It appears to be provided more widely than adaptive education, though there are indications that the corrective programmes are often too divorced from the general education of the pupil; that they are relatively ineffective when assessed on a long-term basis; and that the scale of provision falls lamentably short of the need (Collins, 1961; Chazan, 1967; Cashdan and Pumphrey, 1969; Cashdan et al., 1971; National Association for Remedial Education, 1970; Brennan, 1971; DES, 1971).

Remedial education

In this sub-section the term *remedial education* is used with a more limited, though more precise meaning than in current usage, where it is frequently a generic term which includes, but does not differentiate between *adaptive* and *corrective* education as defined above.

Here, remedial education is regarded as the kind of education required to meet needs which are the result of *learning disabilities*, that is, learning failure which cannot be explained by any reference to inadequacies in the pupil's environmental situation or life experience. Such pupils may be exposed to rich environmental stimulation; they may be in contact with models adequate for normal learning; and they may be exposed to positive, shaping influences in home, neighbourhood and school. Yet they fail to learn normally. Put another way, these pupils are exposed to adequate input at the sensory level, but the input does not contribute to growing and widening experience which itself becomes the basis for more mature or more complex behaviour.

Characteristic of these learning disabilities is breakdown or inadequacy in the pupil's perceptual relationship with his environment, indicating receptive failure, or failure in the *decoding* of sensory information. Or the disability may be in perceptual–motor links, suggesting failure in encoding functions where outgoing neural impulses require translation into muscular action. Clumsy gross motor movement, lack of hand–eye co-ordination, difficulty in keeping eyes in register with a moving object are often indicative of the disabilities, which sometimes appear to rest on the pupil's inability to *match* simultaneous inputs from different sensory channels or to deal with the correct sequencing of continuous sensory inputs. Other characteristics are difficulty in retaining information in immediate, short-term memory which induces difficulty in comprehension and learning; and difficulty in retrieving information from longer-term memory storage. The general result of the disabilities appears as the pupil's uncertain and transient relationship with his environment, one of the main contributors to the behavioural character-istics of hyperactivity, inconsequential disorganization, atten-tion to irrelevant detail and irrational, inconsistent thought. Again, a complicating factor is that though these character-istics are associated with specific learning disability for some children, for many they have a generally depressing effect upon cognitive development as well as upon attainments. Both groups of pupils will need remedial education. The first group need it so that they may overcome or reduce their learning disabilities; the second, especially if they are young, in the hope that appropriate remedial education may promote general cognitive development as well as contributing to the resolution of learning disabilities, so creating circumstances in which they will derive optimum benefit from the adaptive education which they will also require. Pupils who need remedial education include those described in the literature reviewed in chapter 2 as organic, brain-damaged, suffering minimal cerebral dysfunction or exhibiting the Strauss syn-drome, and attention is again directed to Gulliford's caution about the use of these terms (chapter 2, p. 29).

At the time of writing, work in developing programmes of remedial education for the learning disabilities described is limited to a few exceptional special schools, clinics or remedial advisory services. Nevertheless, there is an adequate literature to justify our specific definition of the need and to indicate starting points for the development of remedial education programmes (Strauss and Lehtinen, 1947; Strauss and Kephart, 1955; Gallagher, 1960; Kephart, 1960; Cruickshank et al., 1961; Cruickshank, 1967; Tyson, 1963, 1970; Roach and Kephart, 1966; Frostig and Horne, 1967; Frostig and Maslow, 1973; Tansley, 1967; Johnson and Myklebust, 1967; Benyon, 1968; Chaney and Kephart, 1968; Tarnopol, 1969; Francis-Williams, 1970; Brennan et al., 1972; DES, 1972; Wedell, 1974). The indications are that such programmes will be tightly structured and carefully sequenced, requiring a high proportion of individual instruction in a single, special teacher-to-pupil situation, which will mean the withdrawal of the pupil from some normal group or class activities. But even at this early stage of development it does appear that the remedial programmes will be most effective if conducted against the background of carefully controlled global stimulation provided for the pupil through the wide, varied and exciting activities of general education. Consequently, an important responsibility will continue to rest with the school through its control of the pupil's curriculum. Teachers will also play an increasingly important role in the determination of the pupil's remedial needs as sensitive diagnosis comes to rely more upon information provided from the teacher's observation of the pupil's responses in learning situations. These possibilities go far to justify the new, more precise definition of remedial education, which should alert schools to special pupil needs in an area where educational techniques are new and tentative and where the awareness of special problems is a first, necessary step in the development and refinement of educational methods.

Relationship of adaptive, corrective and remedial education

Adaptive, developmental education provides for education through general, permanent and continuous modification of curriculum content, methods and objectives in order to meet the persistent, general and continuous needs of permanently slow-learning pupils. *Corrective education* provides programmes designed to enable pupils to overcome or reduce learning limitations which arise from missing or inadequate environmental experience and general inadequacies of knowledge or skill. *Remedial education* provides programmes which concentrate on enabling pupils to overcome or circumvent learning disabilities which originate in deficiencies or inadequacies in the processing and using of sensory information as the basis of normal learning. Corrective and remedial education are best regarded as providing temporary programmes which, if successful, may enable some pupils to participate in the normal school curriculum whilst others are enabled to obtain optimum benefit from the adaptive developmental curriculum which will continue to be essential for their appropriate education. The relationships between the different kinds of education are the result of interactions between the different kinds of pupil needs which give rise to them, and to appreciate these relationships it is necessary to understand two important aspects of the interactions. These important aspects of the interactions are, first, that the different kinds of need are not independent; and, second, that the needs are not sequential.

The different kinds of needs are not independent because the fact that a pupil has needs which require corrective education does not necessarily imply that he will not have needs requiring remedial education, adaptive education, or both. The relationships can only be determined on an individual level. One pupil needing corrective education in the area of reading skill but of good general ability may, on successful completion of his programme, be successful in following the normal school curriculum. Another pupil, of poor general ability, may require a very similar programme of corrective reading, the successful completion of which is unlikely to equip him to participate in the normal curriculum but may be essential if he is to gain maximum benefit from the adaptive, developmental curriculum made necessary by his poor ability. Another pupil may prove to have a complex of needs which would require that his curriculum should include adaptive, corrective and remedial education. Such a situation would highlight another aspect of the relationship between the different needs. It was pointed out above that remedial programmes might require a high proportion of work in a special one-pupil-one-teacher situation, which would reduce the time during which the pupil could participate in the wider, exciting and stimulating activities of the general school curriculum. For many pupils, and especially for younger children, this situation might create gaps or inadequacies in experience, knowledge or skill which could result in needs requiring corrective education. And should such a pupil also have limited general ability, the time taken by his remedial and corrective programmes would make it necessary to give special and careful attention to his adaptive, developmental curriculum because of the reduced amount of time available for it. Failure also demonstrates the relationship between the different needs. In the present state of knowledge there is no certainty of success with remedial or corrective programmes and for some children the failure of these programmes may generate a need for adaptive, developmental education which takes account of their continuing learning disabilities and/or limitations. It follows, then, that, far from being independent, the different kinds of needs interact in ways which have importance for the education of the pupil and require careful individual assessment related to curricular decisions which are the prerogative of the school.

The different kinds of needs are not sequential because it is not necessary to assume that needs of one kind must be fully satisfied before attempting to meet other kinds of need. By examining the pattern of a pupil's needs it is possible to propose a balanced curriculum in which, for instance, a pupil requiring both extensive corrective work in reading and also an adaptive developmental programme may continue the activities of this programme through oral, pictorial and other methods which free his education from dependence on reading, whilst at the same time pursuing his corrective programme with the objective of increasing his reading skill. Even where a pupil needs adaptive, corrective and remedial education, a careful study of his needs should make possible anticipation of the needs likely to be created in one kind of education by activities necessary in the others. Such anticipation, intelligently related to curriculum proposals, should result in a balance of activities for the pupil which are calculated to eliminate or minimize the effect of adverse interaction between the different kinds of education.

It would be quite wrong to believe that the need for balanced curricula created by the interrelationships of the three kinds of education is either simple or easy to achieve. It requires for success: careful definition of pupil needs; equally careful assessment of their distribution between the three kinds of education; careful observation and recording of pupil progress as the basis of continuous modification of programmes; and a very high degree of co-operation between the teachers involved in the pupil's education. This is, and must remain, essentially a responsibility of the school and for two very powerful reasons. First, even the most highly specialized remedial teaching must relate to, and be integrated with, the general education of the pupil. Secondly, only teachers in continuous and intimate relationship with the pupil in learning situations are in a position to make the evaluations upon which the successful balance of his curriculum must depend.

Summary

The characteristics of slow learners are reorganized to suggest three different kinds of need which generate different kinds of education.

Adaptive, developmental education which meets wide, general and permanent needs which require continuous modification of curriculum content, method and objectives throughout the school life of the pupil.

Corrective education designed to compensate for gaps or inadequacies in experience, knowledge or skill which create limitations to learning which can be eliminated or reduced by appropriate teaching.

Remedial education designed to eliminate or circumvent

learning disabilities which result from inadequacy or failure in the sensory–perceptual–motor systems which support learning.

Corrective and remedial education are regarded as providing temporary programmes which, if successful, may enable some pupils to participate in the normal school curriculum, whilst others are brought to a position where they can obtain optimum benefit from the adaptive curriculum which they will continue to need. A complicating factor is that the circumstances which give rise to the need for corrective or remedial education, appear, for some children, to have a depressing effect upon general cognitive development, though it is suggested that, if the programmes are started with young children, this effect may, for some pupils, be eliminated or reduced.

The three kinds of education are neither independent nor sequential but interact and create a situation which can be resolved through the provision of balanced, individual curricular programmes in an effort to meet all the slow learner's needs. The nature of the decisions required to achieve the curricular balance make them a responsibility of the school and the information upon which decisions must be based is such that it is only likely to be provided by teachers who are in continuous and intimate contact with the pupils in learning situations.

4 The slow learner after school

The most crucial test of the education of the slow learner is that posed by the transition from school to the wider, working world, revealing, as it does, the pattern of his 'adult' relationship to society and his fellows as well as the emergence of a personal life-style. It is in this area that the curriculum goals of 'personal adequacy' and 'social competence' are most severely tested. Information from the post-school years, critically related to curriculum goals and methods, offers the most promising opportunity for curriculum validation, modification and improvement. There is evidence that an increasing number of schools now follow up their pupils and refine their procedures in the light of the information they obtain: though that information may remain unpublished. In addition, there is a considerable body of published information, though R. N. Jackson (1966, 1968) has criticized its scope and method, largely because of the short follow-up periods of most studies and the lack of precision in their estimates. For the present purpose there are other limitations. Many of the studies originate in the USA and are merely suggestive in relation to British schools. In both British and American studies, it is difficult to separate data relating to slow learners from the total samples.

Studies in the USA: post-school adjustment

An early study in the USA was that by Channing (1932). She showed that the backward group were unemployed to a greater extent than normal school-leavers; they held jobs which were less skilled, and indeed, were seldom employed above the semi-skilled level; the majority were in jobs classi-

47

fied as factory or mechanical work, with some boys in transport and girls in domestic service. Channing related job success to success in practical subjects in school as this factor was related to length of employment, higher wages and greater pay increases since starting work. Nevertheless, employers rated as successful 78 per cent of the work done by boys and 80 per cent of that performed by girls. Kennedy (1948), DiMichael (1950) and Phelps (1956) confirmed the general pattern of Channing's results. In the Phelps study the following variables were related to individuals receiving wages above the median for the group: union membership; rated by employer as doing his share of work well, doing more than expected for his ability, likely to advance, superior general quality of work and good appearance; rated by last special teacher as having good social acceptability and good ability to do his share; IQ above median for group.

Lord (1933) surveyed 230 special-class children in Massachusetts. He found that 82 per cent had no delinquency recorded; 80 per cent were considered to be spending their leisure-time profitably; and 76 per cent were effectively adjusted at home. Abel and Kinder (1942) studied girls from special classes in New York and showed that problems, and factors making for success, were similar at different levels of retardation. Successful girls tended to come from accepting homes and to show traits of self-esteem, patience, willingness to accept some things not liked, and strong work-drive or ambition. Kennedy (1948) found similarity in the marital adjustment of her mentally handicapped and normal groups, though the former tended to have more divorces and step- or adopted children. Compared with the normal group, the retarded showed more anti-social acts, less participation in social activities or membership of civic groups.

C. Ingram (1960) summarized the position in the USA. According to her, the slow learner has limited capacities but can hold employment at the semi-skilled or unskilled level; is likely to earn wages slightly below average; can be successful in home-making; and can make adequate contributions to the community and on his job. This success depends upon the individual's ability to find a suitable job; the degree to which he has developed self-esteem, self-reliance, punctuality, courtesy, industry, obedience, co-operation, steadiness and perseverance; the degree to which his home fosters and develops the above traits; the degree to which he meets tolerance and support at work and in his community (pp. 75-86, 3rd edn). It is difficult to generalize about these studies, but it is interesting to note that in spite of claimed improvements in the education of slow learners there is no outstanding or remarkable improvement in the figures for good adjustment. This is not to say that individuals may not be happier and living richer lives, but if they are, the research suggests that the qualities which support happiness and personal richness for the slow learner are very much the same as those required by all pupils in making the transition from the school to the outside world. Goldstein (1964) in a review of the literature substantially confirms the above summary but warns about changing conditions of employment, due to the reduction in unskilled jobs available, which may bring retardates into more direct competition with their normal peers. He suggests that these conditions call for increased efficiency in the education of mentally handicapped pupils. Wolfensberger (1967) concurs and calls for better quality in research.

Studies in Britain: post-school adjustment

In Britain a succession of studies have examined the transition from school to work, but as they are not specifically concerned with the slow learner it is difficult to isolate from them data relating to less able pupils. So far as this can be done it is now summarized with the warning that it represents the position of secondary modern pupils in general rather than slow learners as such.

Social class aspirations, reinforced by the stratification of secondary education, contribute a crude kind of guidance in relation to the job aspirations of pupils. Less than 10 per cent of leavers are likely to have serious job aspirations and of these no more than two-fifths are likely to achieve the job of their choice. Only one-third of the pupils will have reasonable knowledge of the tasks involved in the job of their choice and about the same proportion will eventually claim to find some satisfaction in their work. Overall about one-third will obtain skilled work, though the proportion varies greatly between different regions of the country. In the first year out from school about one-third will change their jobs at least once and some three, four or even five times. Of these changes about a third will be for commendable reasons but the whole pattern will be marked by a lack of systematic exploration of the employment field. Family and friends figure largely in first and subsequent job choices and may exercise 'influence' in helping to secure jobs. The Careers Advisory Service will place 27-30 per cent of the school-leavers and this group will be biased towards the slow learners or pupils with other difficulties affecting job placement (Ferguson and Cunnison, 1951; Wilson, 1953; Hereford, 1957; Clements, 1958; Paul, 1962; Veness, 1962; Carter, 1962, 1966; Maizells, 1965).

Tansley and Gulliford (1960, pp. 218-21) summarized a number of follow-up studies relating to pupils from ESN special schools. These studies suggest that between 69 and 89 per cent of the pupils had made a satisfactory adjustment to work; most were in unskilled work with a few at the semi-skilled level; there was rapid and high job turnover – 50 per cent changing within three months of leaving school and 20 per cent more than twice, with 37 per cent showing five or more jobs within two years. Failure appeared to relate more to instability and immaturity than to the level of tested intelligence. An overview of this work suggests that a very stable group contributes to the successful outcomes and an exceptionally unstable group to the failures (Brown, 1954; Hargrove, 1954; O'Connor, 1954; Collman, 1956; Atkinson, 1957; Jones, 1957; Taylor, 1957).

Matthew (1963, 1964, 1968) has reported a follow-up of ESN special school-leavers and made some comparison with a secondary modern school sample. In the ESN group employment success was graded complete (44 per cent), partial (14 per cent) and qualified (13 per cent), a total of 71 per cent showing some success: in contrast, the secondary group showed only complete success (97 per cent) and complete failure (3 per cent). A detailed study of the ESN failures (15 per cent) showed that they ranged widely in IQ level and level of reading skill; came from homes varying from squalid to comfortable; had adverse experiences which were not peculiar to the failure group; and seemed to show one handicapping condition disproportionately (maternal overprotection is instanced). Overall employment was lower for the ESN group (74 per cent) than for the secondary group (92 per cent). R. N. Jackson (1968) used a stricter measure of adjustment to employment which showed only 64 per cent of ESN school-leavers making some adjustment to employment; a positive relationship between level of tested IQ and adjustment; and a pattern of unemployment for youths which showed greater instability of employment but less prolonged unemployment than was shown by girls. Examination of these two studies suggests that Jackson's data are of no higher quality than those of Matthew, and it is possible that the studies reflect qualitatively different situations in England (Matthew) and Scotland (Jackson).

Cheshire Education Committee (1963) lists the following job classifications as having been successfully held by slow learners from ordinary schools (number of different jobs in each category given in brackets). Youths held: apprenticeships (10), factory work (23), distribution (10), others (22). Girls held: catering and domestic (8), textile and clothing (6), factory (17), others (15). The qualities making for success are noted as stability of personality and character, general emotional control, ability to get along with fellows, attention to detail and standards and regard for rules and regulations. Conversely, factors associated with failure are listed as personality defects due to emotional instability, failure to adjust to others, unreliability, inability to take responsibility, lack of knowledge or skill, lack of punctuality and absenteeism.

The British Psychological Society (1962) defined the factors which made work adjustment difficult for slow learners as: poor emotional control, resentment against authority, poor educational attainments, lack of general knowledge, lack of vocational training and poor work habits. It was pointed out, however, that research over the previous decade had indicated that many of the characteristics were modifiable or reversible. The value of factory work for slow learners was stressed as suitable because it provided minimum of learning difficulties, variety of unskilled work, opportunity for promotion to semi-skilled work, good wages, good supervision and companion-ship.

Durojaiye (1969) studied three groups of pupils from ESN special schools, backward classes in secondary schools and ordinary classes in secondary schools. Some pupils were still in school and provided information on aspirations; others were at work and provided data on performance. The results of the study indicate that more pupils from the special schools chose unskilled jobs than did pupils in the backward or the ordinary classes; special school pupils appeared to depend more on the school for occupational choice – the others mentioning the influence of relatives and friends most; those at work showed close agreement between the jobs they had aspired to and the jobs they held; and there was no significant difference in the level of occupational adjustment achieved by pupils from the three school sources. Occupational awareness was revealed as one of the most important factors in occupa-tional choice, exercising influence on all school variables.

Wyman (1968) studied forty ex-pupils from the backward classes of a secondary school in Essex. No objective test data were available but pupils leaving school had been subjectively placed on a five-point scale for general school achievement. All the slow learners were in the three lowest grades: C, three pupils; D, twenty pupils; and E, seventeen pupils. Jobs requiring apprenticeship or considerable training were held by 25 per cent of the sample on leaving school; 30 per cent held jobs which required some knowledge and instruction; and 45 per cent went to jobs where no instruction was required. Achievement levels D and E showed $44\frac{1}{2}$ per cent in the unskilled jobs, 25 per cent in semi-skilled and 25 per cent at the level of highest skill. In a period ranging up to three years the 'norm' for job changes in the group was three (32 per cent of the group) and the range upward reached ten, frequent change being associated with low school achievement and low cultural level of the home when subjectively assessed on a five-point scale. The job changes made no significant difference to the job status in the group as a whole, the distribution at the time of the study being the same as at the first job.

Reasons given for changing jobs were interesting and are presented in rank order, equal ranks being in italics: work disliked, poor relations with authority figures, *unsuitable for work, poor relations with workmates, self-improvement,* illness or absence, poor timekeeping, *redundance, accidents, journey too long.* Some of the data from Wyman's study can be compared with those for leavers from ESN special schools with IQ scores from 75 to 87 in a study by Brennan (1972). In this group, which could be expected to overlap in ability with the slow learners from Wyman, the full employment from her group contrasts with the 18 per cent unemployment and 3 per cent unemployable in Brennan's study. Brennan had no cases of employment in skilled work, $43\frac{1}{2}$ per cent at the semi-skilled level and $56\frac{1}{2}$ per cent at the unskilled level. The jobs were more finely categorized in the following rank order of frequency (equal ranks in italics): factory work, catering, cleaning, van/delivery, *animal/land, building,* domestic services, armed forces. Job changes in the two groups gave the same rounded average though exact means were Wyman's 2·15; Brennan's 2·30. In the latter group there was a tendency for lower IQ scores to be associated with more changes of job. Reasons for changing jobs were classified in the same way for both groups; the rank order for Brennan's group is presented with the rank for Wyman's group in the brackets: self-improvement (3), work disliked (1), illness/absence (6), journey too long (8), *unsuitable for work (3), poor relations with workmates (3),* accident (8), *poor relations with authority figures (2), poor timekeeping (7).* Redundancy, ranked 8 in Wyman's group but does not appear in Brennan's data. Perhaps the most interesting differences in the two groups concern relations with workmates and relations with authority figures. In both sets of relationships Brennan's special school group appear to have less difficulty and the order of difficulty between the two sets is reversed. On the other hand, the special school group appear to have more difficulty with the journey to work and to experience more illness and poor attendance.

Also comparable with Wyman's study are those of Collman and Newlyn (1956, 1957) which were conducted in Essex. In these studies 106 intellectually normal pupils, 200 mentally dull pupils from ordinary secondary schools and 125 pupils from ESN day special school were followed up 2-3½ years after leaving school. Over the whole sample the skill-level of employment increases with increases in IQ score. In the two groups from ordinary schools no statistically significant differences were found in the employment of youths and girls; failure-levels in both groups were negligible and similar; and employers listed the reasons for failure or partial success as character deficits, inefficiency, temperamental instability and adverse home conditions. Results for the special school group were similar.

A group of slow learners, 212 boys and 145 girls, were followed up three months after leaving ordinary schools by J. Wilson (1971). Adjustment to work was rated by employers, who found 43·9 per cent of boys and 48·2 per cent of girls above average; 25·8 per cent and 23·7 per cent average; 29·3 per cent of boys and 28·4 per cent of girls below average. Patterns of assessment for *attendance* and *concentration* were similar for the sexes, but boys showed more *keenness for work* and girls greater *ability to follow instructions*. Over the job-categories of skilled, semi-skilled and unskilled, boys clustered towards the first two and girls towards the last two categories. Boys (45 per cent) changed jobs more frequently than girls (43 per cent) but the patterns of changes were similar. Reasons for changing jobs were: failure in personal relationships, lack of job satisfaction, poor job selection, lack of proper induction, unsatisfactory home conditions (mainly assessed by parental attitudes). This rank order remained the same for boys and girls. The study shows occupational failure as related to: social class of the father; home conditions as judged by parental attitudes; size of family and reaction to occupational guidance. All the relationships were statistically significant except for home conditions in the girls' group. Pupil-centred factors in failure appeared as failure in relationships with peers and/or supervisors, poor ability in communication, lack of job satisfaction, negative attitude towards authority, rejection of vocational guidance, inability to adjust to industrial environment and inability to achieve the required level of competence. External factors in failure appeared as inadequate selection procedures, lack of proper work-induction, absence of training facilities, unsympathetic attitudes of supervisors and the failure of parents to recognize the limitation of the pupil.

Tuckey *et al.* (1973) reported on a sample of 291 ESN school-leavers followed up between 1968 and 1971. All the leavers were from special schools and were selected in a way which made the group overrepresentative of multiply-handicapped pupils. If those in sheltered employment are included (43), then 86 per cent of the group were employed at some time. Eighty per cent of the group went into open employment and 26 per cent stayed at their first job for over a year. Three boys were in apprenticeships and one girl in office employment. At the conclusion of the study 78 per cent of the group were still in open employment though earnings were lower than would be expected for a normal group of their age.

Teachers considered that 76 per cent of the group were suitable for further education or training but only 25 per cent were involved in such schemes.

These pupils were more seriously handicapped than most of the leavers considered in this review, but it is interesting to note that, from the limited information available, they do not differ markedly from other, less handicapped, slow learners.

An overview of the above studies does not suggest that there will be any significant differences in the employment adjustment of slow learners when compared with their normal peers. They will, however, tend to hold jobs at a lower level of skill; to change the job more frequently; to work nearer their home; to make more use of the Careers Advisory Service. Compared with ESN school-leavers, slow learners from ordinary schools are likely to have more difficulty with relationships at work but less illness and absence. The factors affecting employment adjustment are not different for the slow learners and can be classified as qualities associated with stability of temperament and character, persistence and consistency.

General social adjustment

Adjustment to employment is, of course, only part of life and general social adjustment arising from participation in social life is at least as important. Unfortunately, data relating to this aspect of the slow learner after school are relatively rare. Tansley and Gulliford (1960) summarize the outcomes of studies and add their own observations to suggest that slow learners have difficulties due to their inability to cope with new situations and people; lack of awareness of sources of useful social information; failure of homes to give them sufficient support; and absence of interesting leisure activities. Matthew (1963, 1964, 1968) has shown slow learners to have fewer friends and less social interaction than their normal peers with a disturbingly higher proportion of lonely isolates. They engage in fewer activities, spend less time outside the home and, unlike their normal peers, appear to prefer passive rather than active occupation. If social competence is considered separately from adjustment, Matthew's slow learners compared unfavourably with his normal group who found his test too easy. Of the slow learners less than half could read above the $10\frac{1}{2}$-year level; complete an application form successfully; calculate amounts beyond £1 (in £.s.d.); find a number in a telephone directory; or understand sick-note procedure. On the other hand, 92 per cent could handle coins efficiently and 74 per cent could calculate efficiently below £1 (£.s.d.); 94 per cent could write their name and address and 60 per cent could address an envelope; 71 per cent could use the telephone and 92 per cent had knowledge of two methods of saving money.

Brennan (1972) examined social behaviour in his ESN school group with IQ range 75-87. In this group 34 per cent had been involved in anti-social behaviour, the incidents in rank order being: stealing from elsewhere, sexual offences, *stealing from home, behaviour to public danger,* and *breaking-in, stealing from work, aggressive behaviour.* Sex offences ranked first for girls and second for youths and accounted respectively for 80 and 57 per cent of incidents. Stealing from home ranked second for the girls and stealing from elsewhere first for the youths. Breaking-in was not recorded for any girls. Friendships were recorded for 82 per cent of the group, a further 5 per cent had positive references to friends and 4 per cent undesirable references: 9 per cent were recorded as being isolates and without friends. Membership of a club was recorded for 3 per cent of the group and 5 per cent had some contact with further education. In general social adjustment 36 per cent were judged well adjusted, 54 per cent adjusted and 10 per cent poorly adjusted, whilst social independence was judged high for 5 per cent, average for 90 per cent and low for 5 per cent.

R. N. Jackson (1970) examined the records of pupils from special schools and classes in a Scottish town. Between the ages of eight and eighteen years 29.8 per cent of boys and none of the girls had records of delinquency – though it is noted that four girls admitted to mental hospital had committed 'moral delinquent' acts. The rank order of classes of offences is recorded as: crimes against property with violence, crimes against property without violence, miscellaneous offences, crimes against the person and malicious damage to property. There was a tendency for delinquent youths to be more intelligent than non-delinquent, and those committing their first offence after leaving school were significantly more intelligent than those offending first during school years. A significant relationship was revealed between delinquency and absence of physical defect, family neglect, abnormal family structure, and occupational instability. Occupational instability was also significantly related to post-school first offences. Recidivism was high, as 59 per cent of the individuals involved reappeared before courts and were again convicted. This study is not directly comparable with that of Brennan (1972) which refers only to post-school years and also includes reported as well as convicted incidents; but together the studies do begin to throw some light on this aspect of the post-school lives of slow learners.

Though the research must be considered inadequate, the picture which emerges is not that of a slow learner with a pattern of social adjustment clearly marking him off from normality. It is a picture of marginal but broad incompetence resulting from a lack of social knowledge, awareness and skill overlaying a degree of immaturity which makes it difficult for the individual to restrain his desires or delay gratification. It is as though reduced intellectual insight into personal problems increases the egocentricity of the individual and results in extremely narrow social assimilation which makes it difficult for the slow learner to learn from his own experience. It is this *social* failure which causes much of the vocational failure of slow learners.

Summary

The inadequate post-school adjustment of slow learners arises from irresponsible behaviour due to emotional immaturity and a tendency to act on impulse; lack of adequate supervision after leaving school; and a lack of understanding, especially by employers and fellow workers. However, around 70 per cent appear to make a successful transition to the working world and with more support and better preparation in school this figure could be increased. The qualities which need to be fostered are those of self-esteem and self-reliance, courtesy, ability to listen to and follow instructions, willingness to recognize the need for help and to seek it properly, friendliness in approaches to others and interest in appropriate leisure activities. School experiences which foster these positive social qualities will contribute more to vocational success than will narrow, specific vocational training.

Preparation for the working world

In this section it is proposed to examine that part of the school curriculum designed to prepare slow-learning pupils for the transition from school to work. This seems natural, following the discussion of the slow learner after school, though it does anticipate the wider discussion of the school curriculum for slow-learning pupils. In one sense, however, there is no such thing as a separate programme of preparation for the working world. The qualities needed by the slow learner, if he is to make a successful adjustment to post-school life, are qualities which are formed and developed over the whole of his school life, keeping pace with his development and becoming richer as he matures. These personal and social qualities are the concern of the *whole* of the school curriculum; many result from the 'shaping' approach to learning, discussed in the next chapter, which will also suggest an approach to planning the curriculum which may assist in the shaping. What 'school-leavers' programmes' can achieve depends entirely upon the success of the curriculum in fostering the knowledge, skills, sensitivities, attitudes and values required by the pupil in meeting the challenge of young adulthood. What the programmes *can* do is to take what the pupil has achieved by his last year in school and help him to direct it in a very special way towards the problems likely to face him in the future. They can do this successfully because they come at a time when the pupil is well orientated towards adult life, highly motivated by the prospect of his entry into it and eager to translate his achievements into the new situations provided by it. Also, in relation to those slow learners who still need to improve their basic skills of literacy and numeracy in the last year at school, the activities of the 'leavers' programme' provide a splendid source of motivation if used with skill by the teacher.

The curriculum and the working world

Kirk and Johnson (1951, pp. 199-225) build their curriculum around areas of experience concerned with: homemaking, occupational education, social relationships and physical and mental health. In addition they suggest (pp. 323-59) classroom procedures which facilitate social adjustment as: teaching procedures designed to foster positive attitudes and mental health; positive pressures towards acceptable social behaviour; pupil involvement in selection of class activities;

the use of socio-drama to develop insight into practical life activities; and the introduction of self-determining activities to give pupils the opportunity to practise the independent management of their affairs. C. Ingram (1960, pp. 341-60) adds recreational pursuits to the areas suggested by Kirk and Johnson. She also sets out in detail a three-year course in occupational education which starts with general awareness of jobs in the community and work in the home, moving on to a consideration of the skills needed in various jobs, workshop relationships, conditions of employment, social security and unions – all based on workshop visits reinforced with planned work experience within the school: in the final stage there is work experience in a part-time job, safety training, job adjustment and related skills of wage calculation, budgeting and savings. Goldstein and Heber (1967) include teaching units on health and safety, social development and adjustment, personal grooming, family living, community living, occupational information and requirements. In addition a special unit on employment includes: the qualities of a good worker; characteristics of jobs and qualifications required for them; job applications; responsibilities of worker and employer; law and custom relating to wages; and self-evaluation in relation to job prospects. In the unit, class instruction is supplemented by visits to places of employment and community agencies concerned with job placement and employment.

In Britain Tansley and Gulliford (1960) were the first to pay detailed attention to the preparation of the slow learner for the transition from school to work. They see this as part of the school curriculum concerned with social competence and dependent upon what has been achieved in personal competence and maturity. Their pre-vocational training programme has seven main areas: (1) industrial visits to introduce variety of working conditions; (2) the introduction of new experiences which enables the pupil to anticipate the demands of adulthood; (3) training in specific aspects of working life; (4) advice on leisure activities and relationships with the opposite sex; (5) guidance on adjustment in the home; (6) personal budgeting; and (7) educational first-aid for very retarded school leavers (pp. 221-43). They also discuss school procedures likely to foster social maturity in the pupil under five headings: (1) fostering in the pupil of feelings of success; (2) learning situations planned to encourage habits of independence and self-direction; (3) carefully structured teaching in areas of self-help, hygiene and courtesy; (4) consistent discipline designed to encourage self-examination and self criticism; and (5) involvement of pupils in rule-making and the ordering of routine at appropriate levels. Tansley and Brennan (1963) have commented upon the above programme, added detail on method and suggested how it could be more closely related to work in basic literacy through the use of English workbooks related to the programme content (Brennan, 1970a).

In a consideration of leavers' programmes in the ordinary school, Brennan (1970b) presented a reanalysis of the curriculum. He saw the sources for curriculum work in an analysis of the demands of society related to an analysis of the situation of the slow learner at school-leaving age, with both these factors related to the problems generated by the contrasts which exist between the ethos of the school and that to be encountered by the pupil in the wider, less protected, post-school world. He indicates how the whole of the curriculum and organization of the school must contribute towards the growth of personal responsibility and good personal relationships and he organizes the specific leavers' programme in five areas of *awareness*.

1 *Social awareness* In this area the pupil must learn to: move about the environment; meet public officials and private persons; make contact with community agencies; communicate by telephone; and use public eating places. Records are kept of time and distance perspectives, ability to use money, ability to seek information and accuracy in communication.

2 *Vocational awareness* In this area the pupil must learn about: job availability; variety of industrial tasks; relationship between persons and occupation; the workshop chain of command and authority; worker customs in workshop and factory; time-sheets, wages, insurance and taxes; trade unions;

job-seeking and job applications. Records are kept which become the basis of counselling aimed at creating realistic job aspirations in the pupil.

3 *Personal-economic awareness* Here the pupil regards himself as a wage-earner and spender. He discovers and learns the prices of common commodities, the essential basis for the simulation of the budgeting for everyday things he will need in later life. He becomes aware of price and value, suitability for purpose as part of sensible purchasing, credit trading and saving. Records show his standard of accuracy and his insight into his own needs and limitations.

4 *Personal adjustment awareness* Here the pupil learns to consider other people in relation to his own actions, with stress on the conditions he may meet at work, in order to help him to appreciate and prepare for the more arbitrary demands he will encounter there. He must also learn to anticipate the new situations which he will encounter as a wage-earner in his own home and as an adolescent with more freedom to handle than in his school-days. Much of this can only be approached through socio-drama, simulation and other such techniques which mark out the contrasts between school and the adult world. The success of the programme here relies entirely on wise counselling and guidance based upon close knowledge of individual pupils and careful recording of the development of insights and attitudes.

5 *Personal responsibility awareness* Successful personal adjustment implies the growth of personal responsibility and the pupil here learns to accept the consequences of his actions. He also must learn of his responsibilities as a citizen and at least become aware of the nature of future responsibilities in relation to his own home and family life. He must develop a critical attitude, within his capabilities, towards mass communications which will affect him in his economic, social and political roles. This area culminates in the beginnings of a concept of service to others to which practical social service schemes make a necessary, concrete introduction. It is in this area, too, that school schemes for pupil participation and self-regulation make a major contribution to the education of the slow learner. Brennan also considers the

contribution which practical, specialist subjects, e.g. wood-work, metalwork, gardening, pottery and housecraft can make to the simulation of work experience in school. And so far as out-of-school work experience is concerned, he lists four pre-conditions for its success as: a preceding programme such as he describes preparing the pupil for work experience; pupils mature enough to benefit from the work experience and not too mature to require it; careful organization and grading of work to relate it to pupil needs; and a realization by the teacher that such school-based work experience is far removed from the *real* experience of work and its associated boredom.

In discussing the contribution which specialist subjects can make to simulated work experience, Knight and Walker (1965) describe a 'factory day in school' designed to serve that purpose. C. H. Jones (1970) describes a similar scheme. Jerrold and Fox (1968, 1971) have documented a work experience course developed in an annexe to an ESN special school and list the following conditions as essential to the success of such courses: working conditions must be realistic; work must conform to industrial standards and be from genuine industrial origins; equipment and machines must be of a type used in industry; each pupil must attend as long as necessary; pupils must not be paid; the person in charge of the unit should have had industrial experience and experience in teaching ESN pupils; and pupils should return to the school on 'day release' pattern for continued tuition in the basic subjects. Wilson (1971) suggests similar schemes. Hart (1969) is doubtful about the value of the more specific job training provided by the simulation of work experience and argues that the social failure which is behind the occupa-tional failure of slow learners justifies concentration on social aspects of the curriculum. When presented with the oppor-tunity to develop a school annexe he rejected work experience and concentrated upon creating a 'home' situation in which pupils could escape from the structure of school, treat the 'house' as their own in arranging, decorating, maintaining and entertaining, develop more freedom in relation to their teachers and spend periods of residence in an environment which they were engaged in creating. In this situation a new meaning was given to the areas of the curriculum concerned with personal and social development and maturity, with, it was claimed, outstandingly positive effects on the pupils and especially on the attendance records of 'difficult' pupils in the experiment. J. Wilson (1971) has also recognized the need to foster social maturity as the basis of social interaction and communication. He suggests the use of school counsellors working with pupils and parents in their homes in pursuit of these objectives, and using the work of Skinner (1970) he indicates the usefulness of 'link' courses between secondary schools and colleges of further education as a means of widening the social experience of slow learners.

Hart is certainly right in stressing the paramount feature of social failure among unsuccessful slow learners, as this appears as a major outcome of the research. Without adequate attention to this factor, work experience could be a waste of the pupils' time, particularly as it reduces the time available for other important curricular areas. In this respect all the programmes described share a weakness. The central feature of the ex-pupil's entry into working life is that he suddenly has to operate in a situation in which he must make a large number of new relationships relatively quickly and learn to sustain them at a somewhat shallow and intermittent level. No programme which involves pupils and staff from the same school, with established relationships, can offer much simulation of this critical situation. This suggests that programmes aimed at the transition to work might be better conducted in a situation which brought together pupils from a number of schools and also new staff. For such programmes, 'centres' may need to be established and it may be that for the more immature pupils experience at such a centre should 'follow on' from the end of formal schooling rather than take up precious time in school when the pupil may be too immature to benefit from the programme. Experimental centres on these lines are now operating. Brennan (1968) has implied that in preparing pupils for the outside world schools tend to concentrate too exclusively on the contemporary world *as it is*. He argues that pupils will be adults in a world much changed from that which they enter on leaving school and if they are to maintain adjustment and vocational competency they must become engaged in a continuous process of readjustment and retraining. Such a situation requires the school to make intelligent predictions about future demands on pupils; it requires attention to teaching methods which will enable the pupil to establish 'learning strategies' which will support future learning, and it makes it imperative that the school should make the establishment of positive attitudes to learning and relearning a central curriculum objective. He argues that the sense of responsibility needed for such attitudes will be fostered by involving pupils in curriculum planning and by exposing them to, and training them in, democratic procedures whilst in school.

The Newsom Report (DES, 1963, pp. 72-9) took up much of the work which had been developed with ESN pupils in special schools and gave it a wider currency in relation to slow learners in the secondary schools. It gave approval to the 'outgoing' course in the final year, the opening of the school to the outside world, the wider use of mass communications in the education of the adolescent and the development of limited 'work experience' schemes under school supervision. More novel were the suggestions of a lengthened school day in the final year to bring school more in line with hours of work in industry and the idea that some pupils might pursue some of their final year studies in colleges of further education. Both these ideas are now being exploited by ESN special schools in the ILEA.

5 Shaping the education of slow learners

The starting-point for the curriculum is the pupil as *he* is and for that reason considerable emphasis is placed upon the teacher's knowledge of the pupil. Equally important is the teacher's knowledge of the personal and social demands likely to be made upon the pupil in the post-school years. In bringing together these sources of knowledge the teacher begins to establish his curricular priorities, his goals and also begins to shape the strategies by which he proposes to attain them. In the process teacher becomes *teachers*, for the strategies must operate over the whole school life of the pupil, involving the school as an institution and, beyond it, the whole system of education as it interacts with wide social pressures. In these respects the relationship between the slow learner and the curriculum is not different from that between the normal pupil and the curriculum. Yet there are often subtle differences. Knowledge of the slow-learning pupil means knowledge of his *inadequacies* and this knowledge often leads to an implicit assumption that the slow learner will continue to function as such with relatively unaltered patterns of strength and weakness. Such an assumption is restrictive in that it underestimates the power of education to enrich the individual and change the pattern of his potential, but it is further restrictive in that it too easily allows the goals of education to be determined from *outside* the process of education as a result of overemphasis of utilitarian demands. In the education of slow learners this restrictive assumption operates more commonly than in the education of normal pupils.

But why do teachers so often adopt a restrictive approach

to slow learners whose very circumscribed situation demands the opposite? In attempting to answer this question it is necessary to examine a major tension in education in a democratic society. Democracy stresses the value of the individual person and has the expression of individuality as a continuing educational aim. But individuality must be expressed with regard to the rights of other persons, and the individual must be socialized so that he, with others, may express his individuality in a manner acceptable in his culture; and also, in a democracy, socialization must contribute to harmony between persons without inhibiting the variety of ideas and attitudes which is required to support social change and development. The tension between individuality and socialization creates problems for educators which are at once subtle and complex. In the education of normal children teachers resolve the tension through the use of teaching approaches which achieve a balance between individual and communal methods and organization. With the slow learner this is more difficult to achieve. In helping such pupils to overcome their learning difficulties, teachers individualize their methods to a point which would be neither possible nor desirable with normal pupils, and this they do within roughly the same time available for education. As a result, the slow learner and his teachers spend much more time grappling with basic skills in individual situations, find themselves short of time in which to establish real and meaningful contact with the wider world outside the school and the pupil often leaves school with (relative to his potential) a surfeit of knowledge and skill but a lack of social and cultural awareness. So the answer to the question is that the restrictive approach to the education of slow learners arises from a failure to establish a correct balance of priorities in their curricula which will allow teachers to meet the special individual needs of the pupils without creating conditions which limit the breadth and quality of their education.

Overview of approaches to the curriculum

At this point it is necessary to present a preliminary overview of approaches to the curriculum for slow learners. The source for this is the summary of Kirk and Johnson (1951, p. 113) brought up to date.

1 Emphasis on sense training using concrete activities leading to the use of tool subjects (Descoeudres, 1928).

2 Emphasis on a 'watered-down' curriculum through the study of traditional subjects at a low academic level (Inskeep, 1926).

3 Emphasis on practical subjects correlated closely and in an organized manner with the basic subjects (Duncan, 1942).

4 Emphasis on social competence and occupational efficiency through 'core programmes' related to 'life functions' (Hungerford et al., 1948; Goldstein and Seigle, 1958).

5 Emphasis on 'units of experience' related to the developmental level of the pupil and designed to secure interest and motivation (C. Ingram, 1960).

6 Emphasis on the development of special programmes related to specific factors believed to cause the learning difficulties, e.g. 'brain injury', visual–motor impairment, perceptual difficulty (Strauss and Lehtinen, 1947; Strauss and Kephart, 1955; Kephart, 1960; Tansley, 1967; Johnson and Myklebust, 1967; Tarnopol, 1969; Frostig and Maslow, 1973).

7 Emphasis on broad 'subject fields', e.g. communication, numeracy, creative activity, social competence etc. (Tansley and Gulliford, 1960; Bell, 1970; A. Williams, 1970).

The approaches in category 6 do not classify with the other categories as they are specific and limited in their objectives and are not usually claimed as representing attempts to provide full education for slow learners. Such a claim could be made for the other six categories and when examined they fall into two groups. In the first group (categories 1, 2 and 3) the curriculum is based upon what it is believed that the slow learner can master during his years of formal education and content is arbitrarily restricted by the assumed limitation of his understanding. In the second group (categories 4, 5 and 7) there is a direct attempt to relate curriculum content to the 'life demands' which the pupil is likely to meet in open society. The first group stresses a basic minimum to be learned thoroughly, usually with too much emphasis on basic subjects resulting in programmes which are arid, repetitive, lacking in excitement and in transfer outside the school situation. The second group stresses variety of activity outside the school situation, rely heavily on project or 'centre of interest' methods, generate much interest but often fail to transfer it back to the school as a motivator of more routine learning in the basic subjects.

Any balanced curriculum must make use of both the above group approaches. In number, for instance, there is a basic minimum of knowledge and skill which the pupil must master if he is to become socially competent and personally adequate. In reading he will require a very carefully graded series of learning situations if he is to establish that skill at an adequate level. In these two curricular areas it is essential that both content and pace of learning are related to the ability of the pupil if he is to experience success. At the same time these slow-learning pupils need to become richer persons, sensitive to their fellows and competent in relating to the society in which they live. The *real* curricular problem is that of accepting the content limitations required to achieve quality of learning in the basic subjects whilst avoiding an educational programme which is sterile, unexciting and inadequate for both personal richness and social competence. This is the central dilemma in the education of slow learners.

Guidelines for the curriculum

In attempting to resolve the above curricular dilemma a useful concept is that of *education for awareness* which was suggested, though not elaborated, by Tansley and Gulliford (1960). To operate with the concept of *education for awareness* the teacher must understand that for each slow learner areas of knowledge can be defined which must be learned with accuracy, permanency and understanding if they are to have any value for the pupil. But the teacher must also realize that beyond these areas are other, wider areas of knowledge where the pupil may be incapable of learning at the above level of *thoroughness,* though he must establish *awareness* of them if he is to relate effectively to his natural and social environment. These areas where learning for *awareness* is necessary are not less important to the pupil than the areas where learning with *thoroughness* is essential; indeed, in certain circumstances, the former may be more important than the latter in the education of slow-learning pupils. Here are some examples. The small amount of numerical and arithmetical knowledge needed to support simple everyday social transactions is valueless unless established at the level of *thoroughness,* but beyond that knowledge the slow learner needs *awareness* of more advanced knowledge so that he may 'relate' to it when he meets it in conversation or in print. Should he fail to 'relate' because of lack of attention to *education for awareness* he may find himself shut out of some social situations or, worse, may reveal his inadequacy in a manner which exposes him to embarrassment or even ridicule. Without the accuracy and permanence implied by the concept of *thoroughness* reading and writing are meaningless, but *thoroughness* is only essential to establish the functions at a simple everyday level. Once that is achieved, it may be more important to expose the slow learner to radio, television and film so that he may learn to use these channels of communication as continuing sources for *awareness* of his world and its people as well as continuing links with literature, drama, music and the visual arts. Similar concepts can be applied to the acquisition of skills. Many basic skills concerned with personal hygiene, eating, dressing, movement, listening, talking, etc. *must be mastered* at a high level of accuracy and permanence if the pupil is to measure up to the norms of the culture. Other skills are not so absolutely essential unless made so by choice or by special situations. Such skills need not be *mastered* though many of them require to be established at a level of *familiarity*: good examples of these are the motor skills of major national games which are established at the *familiarity* level by most males in the population though *mastered* by few. It is the *familiarity* which allows the many to relate to the *mastery* of the few in a way which has become important in the mass culture, and because of this, failure to establish the necessary *familiarity* in the slow learner may restrict his operation in the culture and deny him a useful area of interaction with his fellows.

Though there may well be different levels of *thoroughness* or *mastery* and of *awareness* or *familiarity*, it is possible to place knowledge and skills into one or other of these categories, though there may be some small area of overlap between them. This can be done most accurately when considering individual pupils, for then individual potential can be related to social and cultural demands in defining the objectives for specific learning situations.

To make maximum use of the concepts of *education for awareness* or *education for familiarity* the teacher must recognize that his work in these areas is not separate from that in areas where he is teaching for *thoroughness* or *mastery*. The areas are not separate because of the potential for interaction between them, interaction which can foster motivation and add excitement to the educative experience of the pupil, but interaction which becomes operative through the insight of the teacher who makes positive and active use of it in his work. Here are some examples of the interaction in progress. Teachers of slow learners are well aware of the need to provide finely graded reading schemes, with considerable repetition of the basic vocabulary, if their pupils are to acquire adequate reading skills: but they also know that these conditions, essential to learning, also promote very considerable boredom in the pupil. By organizing work directed at 'awareness' in areas related to reading, skills which have been *mastered* can be used to extend *awareness* and the excitement generated may serve to motivate the pupil to reinforce the mastery or elevate other skills to that level. Variety of experience in the areas of *awareness* and *familiarity* may be used to extend *mastery* in the skills of communication which may open out new possibilities of adding to knowledge which has the quality of *thoroughness*. Such interactions contribute powerfully to the motivation of the pupil, to the reinforcement of learning, and to the transfer of established learning to new situations, all of which are important for slow-learning pupils.

The guidelines summarized

Here, then, is one way to resolve the tension generated by the need to achieve both thoroughness and breadth in the curriculum for slow-learning pupils. First, carefully define the area where learning with *thoroughness* or *mastery* is essential to future personal adequacy and social competence, reducing content to an essential minimum so that the necessary quality of learning may be established without excessive expenditure of time. Second, carefully define the area where learning for *awareness* or *familiarity* is essential if the pupil is to relate adequately and richly to his fellows, to the main streams of human experience and to the social framework within which he must operate. Third, treat neither of these areas as permanently superior to the other, allowing importance to be determined by the needs of the pupil. Fourth, be clear at all times about the purpose of teaching, know in which area the objective resides and develop teaching and learning strategies accordingly. Fifth, cultivate interaction between the areas in order to motivate and reinforce learning, generate transfer of learning, and balance thoroughness and breadth in the curriculum.

Content, method or both?

Though a synthesis has been proposed, it will be noted that it is only stated in terms of a general approach to the curriculum and that the proposal has as much relevance to teaching method as it has to curriculum content. This is the inevitable result of adopting a 'shaping' approach to the curriculum. This shaping means that it is the total learning situation which is important involving, simultaneously, the materials handled by the pupil; the level of knowledge he is expected to attain through them; the process by which the knowledge is achieved; the skills which may be acquired or practised; the social and verbal interactions which are engendered together with the interests and attitudes which cluster around the situation. In this complex situation some of the teaching objectives refer back to previous pupil experiences, others are achieved in the present but many may reside in the future as goals yet to be attained, towards which the current situation contributes for the pupil only readiness experience. It is this 'teaching in time', at once bringing forward and reaching forward, which contributes powerfully to the shaping of the pupil's learning. And that learning will be at different levels. A common group-learning situation may be leading to insight and understanding for some pupils, others may be involved only at the level of *awareness*, whilst for some the main objective may be their involvement in a group activity, opportunity for conversation of the practise of a basic skill. But whatever the level of involvement it will be contributing to the shaping of the pupil's learning. In situations such as these there can be no clear or permanent line of demarcation between curriculum content and teaching method for both are affected by the teacher's objectives as he manipulates and shapes the interaction of the pupil with his learning environment. In such a fluid situation the good teacher must be something of an opportunist, utilizing the immediate situation to move towards his long-term objectives: consequently, he needs to be very clear in his own mind about the nature of those objectives.

The above approach to the curriculum has been generated out of interaction between education for *thoroughness* or *mastery* and education for *awareness* or *familiarity*. It requires a continuing interaction between curriculum content and teaching method, both of which are responsive to interaction between the pupil and his learning environment. To handle this situation the teacher needs clear curriculum objectives, hence the next section will review the attempts which have been made to state the curriculum objectives in the education of slow-learning pupils.

Curriculum content and objectives

In British education responsibility for the curriculum rests firmly within the schools. This is not the place to discuss this principle, but it has one considerable disadvantage in relation to this section, for the curriculum documents developed in schools are seldom published and, consequently, there is little known about this aspect of the education of slow-learning pupils in Britain. Published documents emanate from the DES (1963, 1964, 1972) or LEAS (Cheshire Education Committee, 1956, 1963) and, in keeping with the tradition, tend to be of a general and advisory nature. Some Schools Council publications have a general relevance to work with slow learners (Schools Council, 1965-71) but specific work is only beginning with the project on 'The Curricular Needs of Slow Learning Pupils' which is due to report its findings in 1975-6. In the USA a different tradition has resulted in the publication of curriculum guides by education authorities and also in more detailed discussion of the topic in the literature.

Curriculum literature: USA Examples of the American approach to the curriculum might well start with Inskeep (1926) who proposed specific objectives listed as health, social living, getting and holding a job, thrift and efficient use of leisure-time. In similar terms, the National Education Association (1938) listed specific objectives under the following classifications: objectives of self-realization, objectives of human relationships, objectives of economic efficiency and objectives of civic responsibilities. Featherstone (1951) developed these suggestions more specifically and produced the area designations of: health, vocation, home and family, personal development, social competence and fundamental skills and abilities. To her general objectives of education for achievement in knowledge, occupation, social relations and leisure activities, Martens (1950) added as specific goals: physical health, ease in social relationships, planning and choice in leisure activities, contribution to family and neighbourhood and, later, maintenance of own home, earning to meet necessities of life, and wise spending of salary. These objectives show very considerable overlap with those of C. Ingram (1960) who proposed mental and physical health, working knowledge of tool subjects, worthy home and community life, worthy use of leisure, and adjustment to industry. Kirk and Johnson (1951) attempted to summarize the specialist literature to that date. They listed as agreed objectives: development of social competence; development of vocational competence; development of emotional security and independence; development of good habits of hygiene and sanitation; learning of tool subjects to appropriate level; learning to occupy leisure in a worth-while manner; learning to become adequate members of a family and a home; and learning to become adequate members of a community. Similar objectives were stated in a rather better way by Nickell (1951) who reported the findings of a State group as follows: mastering communication skills; developing a strong body and a good attitude to it; developing satisfactory social relationships: understanding, appreciating and desiring to improve family life; acquiring knowledge of, practise in and zeal for democratic processes; becoming sensitive to the importance of group action for social goals and proficient in the skills; becoming an effective consumer; becoming occupationally adjusted; developing a meaning for life. Seven years later, from the same State, Goldstein and Seigle (1958) produced a more detailed curriculum guide based upon very considerable discussion with teachers of slow learners. This guide divided the curriculum into the following 'life areas': citizenship, communicating, home and family, leisure, management of material and money, occupational adequacy, physical and mental health, safety, social adjustment and travel. The material in the above areas is divided into sections of traditional academic learning under the headings of: arithmetic, fine arts, language arts, physical education, practical arts, science and social relationships. Within these academic sections the material is sequenced on a developmental basis for primary, intermediate and secondary classes. The whole is a very important attempt to provide a detailed framework within which the teacher can organize the learning of her pupils.

Stevens (1958) has proposed objectives in the education of slow learners as learning objectives. He saw the slow learner learning to: maintain physical well-being; live safely; understand himself; get on with others; communicate ideas; use his leisure-time; travel and move about; earn a living; be a home-maker; enjoy life through appreciation of art, dance and music; adjust to the forces of nature; manage his money. Similar points are made by Johnson (1968), who also stresses similarity in goals for the normal and retarded pupil. Johnson organizes curriculum work under the headings of: personal and emotional adjustment; social adjustment; and economic adjustment. These goals are related to stages of education, the early stage being concerned with establishing mental and physical health, widening social experience, promoting readiness activities in relation to visual and aural discrimination, speech and language, quantitative skills, motor skills and familiarity with everyday materials. The middle stage is scheduled to extending proficiency in general living skills and establishing proficiency in the academic skills of reading, arithmetic and the language arts, these latter being accorded much importance by Johnson. At the final stage social and academic skills are to be consolidated, there is to be application of them in varied situations, there is to be the introduction and development of vocational awareness and skills, and there is to be work experience in preparation for the world of work.

In summary it can be said that work in the USA has concentrated on the personal, social and vocational needs of the slow learner, though the needs tend to be stated in wide terms as general aims rather than classroom objectives. Stevens (1958) has summarized the work in a pertinent way. He notes the overlap in ideas, the difficulties generated by differences in terminology, the sometimes 'high flown' language, and the 'over broad' nature of some of the statements. He also stresses the agreement that the general curriculum goals for the slow learner do not differ markedly from those for his normal peers, with whom he has more similarities than differences. He finally concludes that the whole field lacks a clearly worked-out rationale for curriculum evaluation, a conclusion supported by Kirk (1964).

Curriculum literature: Britain   In Britain, the work of Burt (1937) may be regarded as a first and monumental attempt to raise the problems of the slow learner in an objective and verifiable manner. The work established important insights into the intellectual, emotional and social needs of slow learners; described their family backgrounds and neighbourhood conditions; enumerated the many specific difficulties which contribute to their inability to learn; and, in general, laid a thorough and firm basis for the understanding of the slow learner. But Burt was a psychologist, not a teacher. Consequently, though his work is pertinent and central to generating the curriculum for slow learners, he only attempted this in a limited and elementary way, concentrating on those aspects of most interest to the psychologist. On the general curriculum he stressed the limitation of objectives in the academic subjects, though he indicated the need to distinguish between 'the hopelessly dull and the merely backward' (Burt, 1937, 4th edn, p. 608). The aim and outcome was to be to 'make the child an intelligent citizen and a competent worker [rather] than turn him into a sound or accurate scholar' (ibid., p. 609). To this end there would be physical activity to promote health; handwork to provide problems in thinking as well as dexterity; industrial activities designed to direct attention and interest towards possible future employment; cultural activities, mainly music, dancing, drama and art to promote expression and stability; and though classical literature was thought to be beyond slow learners, detective stories are advocated as providing excitement and incentive for thinking and problem-solving. Schonell (1942) built his work upon that of Burt; equally monumental in scope, it concentrated upon pupils with intelligence test scores in the 75-90 range and those with higher scores but specific backwardness in certain subject areas. Schonell limited himself to work in reading, spelling and English composition, though in an earlier study, later revised and expanded, he investigated backwardness in arithmetic (1957). In these specific subject areas, curriculum content is more closely defined than in the work of Burt and there is more detailed attention to teaching method, but the whole discussion revolves around the above basic subjects, though with a quality not exceeded in the literature; it could be read with profit by most teachers of slow learners.

Though both these psychologists contributed valuable impetus to the study of the needs of slow learners, their work had the secondary effect of diverting attention from wider consideration of the curriculum for slow learners. The work of Burt caused teachers to be overconcerned with the historical conditions influencing the pupil's learning difficulties to the neglect, sometimes, of his current needs; that of Schonell led to the overconcentration on the remediation of basic skills to the neglect, sometimes, of breadth and quality in the general education of slow learners.

Duncan (1942) approached the curriculum for slow learners on a wider front. He reacted strongly against the project methods common in the USA and argued that what was good in the project approach could be equally incorporated in a subject approach which would offer the added advantage of providing more carefully controlled learning situations. In selecting the learning situations he utilized the theories of concrete intelligence noted in chapter 2 above. As a result of this combination, Duncan's curriculum embodied the following subjects: handwork and craft; paper and cardboard work; woodwork; needlework; domestic subjects – housewifery, cookery, laundry-work; art; country dancing; physical education; gardening and rural studies; English; number and mathematics; history and geography. Within each subject area very carefully graded learning steps were organized, based, not upon the logic of the subject-matter, but upon the needs of the pupils as revealed by close study. The subjects themselves are loaded in the direction of practical activities, consistent with the focus upon concrete intelligence and providing for learning through things seen, touched, handled or heard rather than through descriptive verbalizations. But Duncan was not just interested in 'doing'. The activities of the children were planned in a way which emphasized the observation of relationships and processes, directed attention to sequences and stimulated relational and sequential thinking by the pupil. Duncan claimed that this approach in the practical subjects established learning skills which were transferred to the more academic subjects, particularly English and mathematics, and that there was also transfer of motivation.

It is not easy to evaluate the contribution of Duncan to the education of slow learners. He certainly examined in detail the steps in the presentation of the subject-matter to be learned by the pupil and he presents them carefully in his book (1942), which should be studied. And though his analysis of the pupil's learning is global in the sense that it takes account only of 'type' of intelligence, he was, nevertheless, moving towards an approach to teaching not unlike that advocated by more recent writers who have stressed the need for 'structure' in presenting learning situations to slow-learning pupils. Whether or not his methods improved 'relational thinking' or 'developed intellectual abilities' in his pupils must remain an open question, as must his claim that skills were transferred amongst the pupils' activities, for he presents little substantive data on these points. More serious is the absence from his curriculum of practice or concepts relating to the fostering of personal adequacy or the cultivation of social competence and maturity. One has to assume that Duncan believed that by improving intellectual function in a way which facilitated the transfer of learning and skill the pupils would resolve their problems in these areas for themselves. This is suggested by his statement of personal belief 'that the attainment by each child of his maximum potential intellectual efficiency through the cultivation of good mental habits would result in an increased measure of human happiness' (ibid., p. 9).

Both Baron (1938) and Highfield (see Hill 1939) had anticipated Duncan in ther subject approach to the curriculum for slow learners, though neither related the curriculum so firmly to a theoretical model of the child's thinking. Baron kept very close to basics, including only reading, arithmetic, writing, physical education and handwork in his curriculum. Highfield, however, paid some attention to personal development of the pupil and also advocated project methods within her basically subject-orientated curriculum.

During the late 1940s the Cheshire Education Committee, in its Development Plan, rejected the segregation of slow learners into special schools and determined to provide for their education in the ordinary primary and secondary schools. To assist the schools, a joint advisory committee of authority representatives, headteachers and county advisory staff considered the needs of 'dull' pupils at both the primary and secondary stages of education, the results of their deliberations being embodied in two publications (Cheshire Education Committee, 1956, 1963). Both these publications show a predominantly subject-orientated approach to the curriculum. Common to both primary and secondary stages are: English, arithmetic, art, craft, music, history, geography, religious instruction and physical education. Additional subjects at secondary level are: science, domestic science, woodwork, metalwork, rural studies and drama. Nature-study is included for primary pupils, apparently leading to the secondary level science. At both levels some attention is given to personal development through the inclusion of social training for primary pupils whilst secondary pupils have sex education and preparation for employment included in their studies. There is some slight reference to projects as a method, for primary pupils in arithmetic (1956, p. 37) and history/ geography (pp. 142-52); and for secondary pupils in religious instruction (1963, p. 131), art (p. 180) and craft (p. 187).

In general, the approach in these curriculum outlines (Cheshire Education Committee, 1956, 1963) is very firmly that of academic subjects watered down to meet the needs of slow-learning pupils. However, in social training, sex education and preparation for employment there is some move to relate content and methods to the personal needs of pupils, to suggest that subjects might be grouped or taught in a way which might foster personal development, and to indicate, albeit indirectly, the behaviours and attitudes which should be established in the pupil.

Without doubt, the most significant work on the total *education* of slow learners to appear in Britain is that of Tansley and Gulliford (1960) which has influenced all subsequent work. These authors outline two general aims in the education of slow learners. The first aim, of *personal adequacy*, includes the development of well-being through physical and mental health, the achievement of vocational competence, the realization of cultural potential and the acquisition of the basic skills and habits which make the others possible. The second aim, *social adequacy*, includes the abilities and attitudes needed for good social relationships, and the awareness of the duties, rights and privileges which make possible good citizenship. Subsidiary aims for the teacher of slow learners are listed as the fostering in the pupil of self-confidence, self-knowledge and good work habits. The curriculum is seen as having three aspects, the logical, the psychological and the social. Tansley and Gulliford regard the logical approach as the traditional one, largely based upon the internal logic of subject-content. They stress the great need for teachers of slow learners to consider the psychological aspects through attention to the pupil's personal needs and his readiness for learning: the social aspects they see as important because of the increasing demands made on the slow learner as society becomes more complex. In considering the *organization* of the curriculum, Tansley and Gulliford face the dichotomy of the subject *v.* project approaches (1960, p. 101):

> If the curriculum content is compartmentalized into subjects, it is less easy to provide those broad experiences and real-life situations which are so necessary. The importance of social education may be overlooked. If correlation is emphasized, the basic subjects are likely to suffer because of difficulties of control and continuity; teaching may tend to become subservient to the project and not related to the individual.

They suggest a curriculum with two interdependent parts consisting of a central core of language and number with a periphery of useful knowledge about the environment, creative activities and practical interests: 'As the core develops, so the periphery widens, and as the child achieves command of the essential tools of learning he realizes their usefulness. The interplay between core and periphery becomes more sensitive and apparent' (ibid., p. 101). The reader will recognize here the beginning of the concept which was spelled out in more refined detail in the early part of this chapter. For Tansley and Gulliford the core is organized around language, a grouping of reading, spelling and written expression, number, the practical subjects – craft, home-making, physical education, and religious education. The periphery develops around creative work – seen as contributing to intellectual and emotional development as well as the aesthetic; education for social competence; and a fostering of the growth of knowledge and awareness of the human and natural environment.

Tansley and Gulliford (ibid., pp. 90-8) recognize that for the slow learner content must be related to teaching method. They enunciate what may be regarded as important principles of teaching slow learners by stressing individualization of teaching, the use of appropriate methods of learning, the importance of learning readiness, the need for good pupil-motivation, concrete learning (leading to concept formation and growth as a result of carefully graded work), continuous assessment of progress and frequent consolidation to ensure that progress is real.

Significant though it is, the work is not without its weaknesses. Though it indicates the need to help the slow learner to focus and integrate his learning it offers little practical help to this end and the curriculum is discussed largely in subject terms. Pupil records are discussed mainly in relation to the basic subjects and skills in them, with insufficient stress on recording in the peripheral areas in order to shape the growth of awareness and concepts. Though the need for transfer of learning to immediate and contemporary social situations is stressed, there is neglect of the need to teach in a way which encourages the pupil to acquire 'learning strategies' which will transfer to learning in a more distant and different post-school world. Also, in stressing, rightly, the need for the education of the slow learner to be 'child-centred', it is possible that Tansley and Gulliford have allotted insufficient attention to the essentially *deliberate* nature of formal education. Consequently, the reader may be left unaware that some of the essential learning experiences for the slow learner may have their importance, not in school, but in the future – a future which the pupil is too immature to understand or analyse. The recognition, selection and inclusion of such experiences in the curriculum *must* be a function of the teacher and *should* be a conscious and deliberate function. It is not that the above concepts are not present in the work of Tansley and Gulliford: it is, rather, that the balance of the discussion is such that the reader may overlook their significance.

Most subsequent writers on the curriculum for slow learners have been influenced by Tansley and Gulliford and have adopted their principles, though they may have been more specific in relation to methods. Segal (1963) made a specific attempt to differentiate the curriculum between the primary and secondary stages in the ordinary schools. At the first of these stages he organizes the curriculum around mental health – permeating every aspect of the work: social adjustment and maturation; applied communication skills – including 'quantitative' thinking and skills; group and individual safety training; group and individual health training and habits; physical education; and recreation and leisure training. At the secondary stage health training and habits are replaced by health and sex education; preparation for citizenship and vocational education are added, but otherwise the organization and grouping remain as at primary level (ibid., pp. 32-50). Differentiation within the curriculum was also indicated by Cleugh (1961) who collected and edited contributions by various authors which she published as three volumes dealing respectively with primary, secondary and special schools. This work indicates a curriculum based upon grouping of subjects showing: basic skills – speech, reading, arithmetic, with play included for young special school pupils; expressive work – art, music and drama; physical education and health; social, moral and religious education; environmental studies; handicrafts; housecraft; and use of leisure. This was not such a deliberate essay in curriculum differentiation as that of Segal and both might claim that they were primarily concerned with broad content and method. This would certainly be true of Bell (1970) who organizes his curriculum around language, reading, spelling, written work, mathematics, social education, practical and artistic activities, training for leisure and preparation for employment: each 'subject' being discussed primarily in terms of basic content and method. However, he also contributes a useful discussion on the place of 'units of experience' in the education of slow learners (pp. 154-64). In the selection and planning of such units he suggests the following questions as likely to resolve their essential aims and purposes: is it of real and vital interest to children? will the unit create need for the use of basic tool subjects? is it possible to involve children with different levels of attainment? are real, concrete, first-hand experiences involved? how far will children work together, or work with people outside school? will there be opportunities which may help to develop qualities of self-reliance, self-confidence or independence? 'Units of experience' are specific instances of projects or centres of interest, and all will increase in value in the extent to which the criteria suggested by the above questions are satisfied. Bell also considers the nature of experiences provided and stresses the importance of first-hand, direct sensory experience of real things and situations, second-hand experience through stories, pictures, films, etc., and the value of experience through expression in speech, writing or other creative activities. Cleugh (1961), Segal (1963) and Bell (1970) have added methodological point to the principles enunciated by Tansley and Gulliford (1960), but all four sources fail to make clear the behavioural objectives which should be the concern of curricular work and they are, consequently, hazy about the relationship of curricular considerations to the development of children.

The specific, behavioural aspects of the curriculum have been given more attention by Gulliford (1971). He has attempted to specify, albeit in general terms, the behavioural tasks which face slow learners at different stages of their development and he has related these to the stages of education. The slow learner at the infant stage is seen as engaged in coming to terms with people and things in his environment; with movement, for its own sake and as part of exploratory experience; with verbal communication as a regulator of the above processes. It may be necessary to help him to learn to play, and he will certainly require specific help in improving his perception, his fine motor skills and their application in dressing, feeding and other areas of self-help. At the Junior school stage the behavioural objectives are stated more specifically as: learning to be a member of a group, acquiring positive feelings towards self through success and achievement, developing the ability to play and learn, developing thinking and language, finding means of expression through the creative arts and movement, increasing awareness and knowledge of the environment, and achieving readiness for more formal learning in basic educational skills. The tasks at the secondary stage are seen as: consolidation of basic skills in verbal communication, reading and writing; the development of independent skills in these areas; the development of social competence in home, family and peer groups; the preparation for competent behaviour in the outside world in general and in place of work in particular (Gulliford, 1971, pp. 74-80). A similar scheme is outlined in *Slow Learners at School* (DES, 1964, pp. 56-9), which also adds, at the secondary level, adjustment to a longer school day and hard physical work. The same source evaluates the traditional subject areas in relation to the curriculum for slow learners (ibid., pp. 59-64). Primacy is given to spoken language over either writing or reading, objectives in the latter areas being realistically related to the abilities of the pupils; objectives in mathematics are similarly circumscribed and the need for quality and transfer in learning is emphasized; creative work is given objectives beyond expression in reduction of frustration and its contribution to calm, confident and constructive attitudes; and the value of movement to spatial competence and social poise is remarked upon. History, geography and science are seen as having little place in the curriculum of the slow learner except in very practical terms relating to common everyday experience and a similar view is taken of religious education, the value of which is seen as communicated in the life of the school rather than by specific teaching. In a section on learning to live (ibid., pp. 65-72) there is considerable stress on the pupil acquiring behaviours which foster personal responsibility contributing to vocation and family life; attitudes of generosity, honesty and reliability;

discrimination in social relationships; sensible procedures in personal and family hygiene and good health for both girls and boys; adequate knowledge of and contact with resources for positive leisure activities. These accounts (Gulliford, 1971; DES, 1964) add a needed behavioural content to the discussion of the curriculum for slow learners, though it is possible that the latter source is *too* restrictive in its view of the extent to which history, geography and science can contribute to their education. It is doubtful if any person can be socially competent without some ability to weigh the objectivity of evidence, without some knowledge of development in the affairs and institutions of men, and without some knowledge of the interdependence of people in different parts of the world and in different cultures. Many slow learners *can* begin to operate with these concepts if they are introduced in appropriate learning situations and developed over time consistent with the increasing maturity of the pupil; further, work in these areas may be necessary in order to assist the pupil in establishing *positive attitudes* towards learning and the possibility of *intuitive* thinking at a more mature level (Bruner, 1960). This is not to say, of course, that the traditional subjects of history, geography and science must be *taught* to slow learners in an arid, traditional way: rather is it that the slow learner should have some contact with the concepts from these traditional subjects which are important if he is to relate himself realistically to his fellows and to the world in which he must live with them.

The Newsom Report (DES, 1963) adopted a position closer to that implied by the above criticism of *Slow Learners at School*. Newsom saw the curriculum for slow learners in terms of: (1) practical subjects – art, music, physical education, wood- and metal-work, technical drawing, housecraft and needlework; (2) science and mathematics; (3) humanities – English, history, geography, religious instruction and possibly a second language. This choice of subject-orientation was deliberate (para. 353) where it received what must be one of the most pathetic justifications in the whole of educational literature, 'A boy or girl can at least come home and say what his lesson was ... a value which ought not to be sacrificed.'

The report concerned itself almost entirely with curriculum content, again deliberately (para. 353), and though it rejects traditional examinations as measures of what pupils have achieved, it fails to define with any clarity the behavioural outcomes of the proposed curriculum. The main contribution of the report to teaching methods was to stress the need to make school work relevant to life outside the school, thus encouraging the development of outward-looking activities which have been described as 'life adjustment courses'. Some such courses, rapidly and uncritically launched, have been criticized for their lack of conceptual content and their failure to examine in depth some of the human situations in which pupils become actively involved, with the result that they tend to verge upon 'indoctrination' (Lawton, 1970).

Working Paper No. 2 (Schools Council, 1965) takes a broader view than Newsom towards the *real* education of slow learners and has generated work which, though intended for a population wider than slow learners as defined in this study, should nevertheless promote interesting experiments within our field. The paper challenges the view that slow learners are not interested in ideas and cannot handle them; that they cannot handle abstractions; cannot verbalize; are only interested in people or concrete situations; and that they make choices only by comparing immediate satisfactions. This challenge is justified by reference to successful experience with slow learners who have continued in school for a fifth year, from the experience of Further and Adult Education, and from the experience in primary schools that 'practically all pupils can acquire insight into abstract ideas and a capacity to work with them (particularly by oral means) if doors are opened through the use of teaching methods which build on pupils' present experience and supply new forms of experience which help them to discover for themselves the power of their own minds.' The contention is that the coming of a five-year course for slow learners will open up new possibilities which are not attainable in a four-year course. Such a course was seen as requiring consistent, organic unity which would be provided by focusing on the human situation, man in society, his needs and his purposes, and extending the discipline beyond Newsom by bringing in concepts from economics, sociology, psychology and anthropology.

The direct outcome of the working paper (Schools Council, 1965) is seen in the following projects.

1 *Nuffield Foundation and Schools Council Humanities Project.* This is preparing classroom material designed to enable pupils to explore 'controversial areas of human concern'. Those chosen are : war and society, education, the family, relations between the sexes, poverty, people and work, law and order, living in cities and race.

2 *Schools Council Secondary School Mathematics Project: Mathematics for the Majority.* This is producing teaching materials intended: to provide mathematical experience which will encourage powers of judgment and imagination; to give pupils some understanding of the mathematical concepts behind everyday numeracy; to remove barriers which separate mathematics from other subjects in the curriculum; to enable pupils to appreciate in some measure order and pattern in their environment.

3 *Nuffield Science Teaching Project: Science for the Young School-Leavers.* This is producing carefully structured material using open-ended experiments relating to the following themes: interdependence of living things; continuity of life; biology of man; harnessing energy; extension of sense perception; movement; using materials; and the earth and its place in the universe.

4 *Schools Council Project: Geography for the Young School-Leaver.* This is producing schemes and materials for use in subject or interdisciplinary work with average and below average pupils of fourteen to sixteen.

5 *Schools Council Moral Education Project.* This is devising curricular materials and methods to help pupils adopt a considerate life-style in which they take account of the needs, interests and feelings of others as well as their own.

Information about the progress of the projects, and about the availability of project materials may be had from: The Information Officer, The Schools Council, 160 Great Portland Street, London W1N 6LL. Another Schools Council team has examined the use of published project materials with slow-learning pupils. Also of some relevance is Working Paper No. 27 (Schools Council, 1970a) which deals with the education of socially disadvantaged pupils, a population which overlaps considerably with the slow learners of this study. Most of the paper is given over to an analysis of their problems, but there is description of some current practice (pp. 31-44) and some consideration of curriculum (pp. 62-86). Again there is little indication of what the curriculum should *achieve*, but the general aims are usefully stated as the need to foster *competence* of an essentially social nature, *confidence* as a more personal thing, and *co-operation* which is active and democratic and involves the pupil in the school community. There has been criticism of the vagueness of much of this paper, which certainly does not cut straight to the heart of its matter. Similar comments have been directed at Working Paper No. 11 (Schools Council, 1967a) which attempted to translate Working Paper No. 2 into classroom terms and describes four approaches to the development of an area of inquiry.

Curriculum development and the slow learner An overview of the literature on the curriculum for the slow learner shows a movement away from an exclusively subject-orientation towards a position where the curriculum is concerned with the slow learner as a person and with his personal relationship to his social and natural environment; in other words, towards a concern with his behaviour. Given this position, what is surprising is the apparent lack of concern with the *behavioural* outcomes of the curriculum. These are rarely discussed except in the most general terms, so general, in fact, that most of the statements apply just as much to *all* pupils as they do to slow-learning pupils. Equally surprising is the absence of rigorous attempts to subject work with slow learners to detailed analysis by the principles of modern curriculum design. (Wheeler, 1967). An exception to this is P. Taylor (1970) who, in relation to compensatory education, has proposed the following scheme: (1) definition of the general aims of education; (2) definition of general objectives; (3) translation of general into specific objectives; (4) itemizing of learning experiences required for the achievement of specific objectives; (5) the translation of these into organized topics and themes which can be handled in the classroom. Gulliford (1971, pp. 26-8) has applied the scheme (stages 1-4) to slow learners at the primary stage and he suggests that the exercise would be worth while even if taken only as far as specific objectives with some account of how they might be achieved 'since it is apt to bring to notice purposes which have not been consciously formulated or which receive insufficient attention' (ibid., p. 27). This is certainly true, but the heterogeneity which exists among slow learners, together with their differential rates of development, requires a more elaborate but at the same time more flexible scheme. Such a scheme will now be outlined.

Statement of aims

These general statements do not differentiate between slow learners and normal pupils because they consist of statements, within philosophical/ethical frames of reference, of the ideal of being human in a particular human society. Unless slow learners are *not* human, or live in a *different* society, there is *no* reason why statements about their education, at this level, should differ at all from statements about the education of *all* children. Yet these statements are important starting-points for the curriculum because they contain our basic values or priorities which give purpose and direction to all which follows. It might be truly said that at this level special education does not exist.

Statement of general objectives

At this level it is necessary to make general statements about the knowledge, skills, sensitivities, attitudes and values which pupils must acquire if the aims of their education are to be satisfied. Here *these* pupils must be considered in *these* situations: account must be taken of the generalized personal and social difficulties which may limit the acquisition of the behaviours enumerated above. At this level the frames of reference have become psychological and sociological and the focus moves from the generalized, mature ideal to the generalized, immature, imperfect slow learners. It is at *this* level that special education begins to have meaning. The first statements to be made will be of *terminal* objectives, the behaviours *expected* at the end of a curriculum extending, perhaps, over years. But because the process of education is prolonged, it will be necessary to formulate *intermediate* objectives, statements about the behaviours to be expected at certain critical points in the education of the pupils, points which should relate in a logical way to phases in their personal development. Because these statements are *generalized*, and because slow learners will not all enter the curriculum at the same point, nor bring to it the same potential, it is important to remember that the above statements must all remain *approximate*, that is, they must be regarded as guiding and shaping work with individuals rather than determining or imprisoning them and they must also be regarded as the best statements which can be made *at the time they are made* and consequently subjected to refinement and revision in the light of experience. It will not be possible to be more specific than this at above the classroom level, for only there, where the individual learner and his circumstances are paramount, can *specific* objectives have any meaning, and then only in interaction with the content and methods which together constitute learning experiences. Nevertheless, within the school, the generalized objectives, terminal and intermediate, are important. They provide the essential framework which supports the teacher in the classroom, the structure which liberates him and allows him to operate with maximum creativity in shaping the learning of individual pupils.

Content and method

With slow learners content and method continually interact in the 'shaping' approach described earlier in the chapter (p. 72). Guided by aims and objectives, the interaction creates learning situations tested by the meaning they have for pupils; by the number of behavioural objectives to which they contribute (knowledge, skill, sensitivities, attitudes); by the possibilities they offer for organizations into topics, themes, centres of interest, etc., which allow for adequate revision, concept formation, enrichment, etc.; by the opportunities they offer for measuring and recording pupil progress towards the behavioural objectives. These are the tests the teacher must operate in the classroom and he, also, will need to apply the plan of aims, objectives, terminal and intermediate, to his classroom activities where the *specific* objectives, unattainable at previous levels, become not only real but essential. It is at this classroom level that the teacher must be aware of the location of the teaching–learning objectives in relation to the areas of thoroughness or awareness discussed on pp. 69-72 and he should realize that, consistent with the 'shaping' approach, many of the behavioural objectives which reside in the areas of sensitivities, attitudes or values will depend for their attainment more upon *how* the pupil learns than upon *what* he learns. In other words, there are circumstances in which method becomes more important than content.

Evaluation

Evaluation is a term which includes assessment in the way that assessment includes measurement. As a result of the learning experiences presented in the curriculum, has any change taken place in this pupil? If so, in what direction is the change? Has the pupil established the behaviours defined in the expected objectives? If not, is his progress towards them satisfactory or unsatisfactory? The first three questions can be answered on the basis of assessment or measurement, dependent upon the nature of the behaviour. The fourth question involves evaluation if it is to be answered. Measurement or assessment will only indicate the nature and extent of the change, whether or not it is satisfactory requires that the change be related to the total circumstances of the pupil, including the teaching he has received: this is the process of evaluation. It is a process in which the *actual* behavioural outcomes of teaching and learning are constantly being compared with the *expected* outcomes. There is also another aspect to evaluation. The aims, objectives, contents and methods of the curriculum must also be subjected to it. A pupil may fail to attain the expected objectives because they are inappropriate for him or because insufficient time has been allowed for his learning. The failure may even be due to inefficient teaching, inappropriate method, or even unsuitable content in the curriculum. Evaluation itself may be at fault if learning intended at the level of awareness is evaluated on the basis of thoroughness. Evaluation of the curriculum process itself is required if such issues are to be resolved. None of this can occur in the absence of careful and continuous *recording* of the learning situations in which the pupil has been placed and of the behavioural outcomes established by him; such recording is vital if the learning of the pupil is to be shaped from the classroom situations, through the intermediate objectives to the terminal objectives.

Feedback and pupil involvement

The process of evaluation is wasted if the information is merely recorded and no further action is taken. The whole purpose is that of refinement of the curricular process, of education; consequently the outcomes of evaluation must feedback as action in relation to the process or the pupil, or both. This is usually seen as a teacher responsibility, and so it is, but part of that responsibility is for the involvement of the pupil in the evaluation so that he, too, can understand it and make use of the information in modifying *his* own behaviour. This will be more efficiently achieved if the pupil is also involved in the formulation of curriculum objectives, at least to the point where he has some understanding of them appropriate to his level of maturity. Acceptance of objectives and knowledge about results are known to be powerful motivators of pupil learning: both work most efficiently in relation to the principles of involvement and feedback. But feedback has another relationship to the curricular process. The levels of general aims, general objectives, content and method and evaluation have been discussed as separate levels. In practice there is constant feedback between them. Aims shape objectives (and indeed may be shaped by them – a constant danger of means superseding ends); objectives influence the choice of content and method, but feedback from consideration of the latter often leads to refinement or alteration in the former; evaluation is determined by the behaviours to be assessed, but where there is choice of behavioural objectives considerations of how to evaluate may well influence the choice. So from level to level and through the levels there is constant interaction based on continuing feedback, indeed, a circular rather than a linear process; or better, a spiral process which emphasizes the continuing interaction between the levels.

It should be noted that the above outline is in no way a curriculum *plan*. It is, rather, an outline of an approach to curriculum *planning* and *development* which could lead to enhancement of the quality of the education of slow-learning pupils. It owes much to modern work on curriculum development (Taba, 1962; Wheeler, 1967; P. H. Taylor, 1967) which seems relevant to the education of slow learners because, (1) in the education of such pupils the interaction between knowledge and behaviour is of critical importance and should be of continuing concern for their teachers; and (2) the review of literature on the curriculum for slow learners indicates an absence of rigorous attempts to define their curricular needs in verifiable, behavioural terms.

Applications: adaptive, corrective and remedial

Throughout this discussion of the curriculum, it will have become clear that the consideration of the curriculum relates most directly to those slow learners whose needs require adaptive, developmental education. This is because, for such pupils, whatever needs they may have for corrective or remedial education, the breadth and quality of their education depends upon the resolution of the problems which they present in the area of adaptive, developmental education. Consequently, their education must be entirely a school responsibility, requiring, as it does, continuous shaping and guidance by teachers in continuous contact with their pupils. There can be no overlooking of the need for such teachers to scrutinize and evaluate their work along the lines indicated in the above discussion. Yet the same approach to curriculum planning is equally applicable in corrective and remedial education. In these, the teacher is usually concerned with the limitations or disabilities of individual pupils or of small homogeneous groups of pupils, and his contact with pupils may be limited through a withdrawal system or through teaching in a 'clinic' or a 'centre'. But compared with adaptive education, the problems presented in corrective or remedial education are less wide or varied, are likely to respond to teaching in a shorter period of time, and for their solution require terminal behaviours which can be more precisely defined. In good corrective or remedial work the general aims and objectives should derive from the wider curriculum which is proposed for the pupil, while the plans for corrective or remedial teaching approximate closely to the level of *specific objectives* suggested above as the concern of the teacher in the classroom. By its nature corrective or remedial work is more limited than teaching in an adaptive curriculum because it has an essentially *enabling* function. These circumstances make the direct application of the suggested approach to curriculum planning in corrective or remedial education a less complex task than in adaptive education, but an equally essential task. It is essential because the touchstone of successful corrective or remedial work is efficiency, defined as the achievement of terminal behaviours in the shortest possible time in order that the pupil may, as soon as possible, derive full benefit from his normal or adaptive curriculum. Such efficiency can be made more certain by the application of the planned and deliberate approach which is the outcome of the suggested method for curriculum planning and development.

Summary

Because of their learning difficulties, slow learners are often required to spend a disproportionate amount of time in

ic knowledge and skills with the result that
and social education is narrower and less rich
t have been. To avoid this it is proposed that
re learning must be for *thoroughness* or *mastery*
educed to an essential minimum, so that the
requ.... ality of learning can be established without excessive expenditure of time, and that areas of learning for *awareness* or *familiarity* be planned into the curriculum to ensure
that the pupil establishes rich contact with his social, cultural
and natural environment. It is stressed that there is no
natural superiority accorded to either of these kinds of learning, for the relative importance is determined by the needs
of the pupil and interaction between the areas may be used
by the teacher to motivate learning, promote the application
of knowledge and skill and facilitate the transfer of both to
new situations.

Statements of aims and objectives in the education of slow
learners show an increasing concern with the personal and
social development of the pupil and with the demands likely
to be made upon him in future family, social and vocational
life. Nevertheless, method still remains generally subject-
centred though there is an increasing trend towards making
use of situation-centred approaches in projects, centres of
interest, etc.

The review of literature shows that the techniques of
modern curriculum development and design have not been
widely applied to the curriculum for slow learners. The tech-
nique is outlined as the reduction of general curriculum aims
to statements of behavioural objectives at intermediate and
terminal points in the curricular process, though it is stressed
that such statements must be regarded as approximate. Such
a curriculum structure should assist the teacher to state
specific classroom objectives for his pupil and enable him to
select learning experiences through which the pupils should
attain the objectives. The outline emphasizes the importance
of recording, evaluation and the feedback of information at
all points in the curricular sequence. It is also suggested that
there is a place for the involvement of the pupil in the process in order to enhance his motivation and to enable him to

use the information as the basis for the modification of his own behaviour. Clarity of terminal and intermediate objectives in the curriculum is seen as essential if the teacher is to use the total learning situation in order to continuously 'shape' the development of the pupil in an on-going process of interaction.

Further reading

General

The extensive bibliography will direct the attention of readers
to sources in which they may follow up points and extend their
reading on specific interests. But more recent work on learning
disabilities demands for its full understanding more knowledge
of the biological, physiological and neurological aspects of
behaviour than has commonly been communicated in teacher
education. A thorough introduction to this background is in
The Biological Bases of Behaviour, edited by N. Chalmers, R.
Crawley and S. P. R. Rose, published by Harper & Row for The
Open University Press (1971). In a series of readings the book
discusses the structure, function and development of the nervous
system; sensory processes and perception; emotion and motivation; learning; memory and intelligence; social behaviour and
some interesting speculations on the brain–mind problem.

Slow learners: definition and extent of the problem

A good general introduction is that by Phillip Williams, chapter
16 in *The Psychological Assessment of Mental and Physical
Handicaps*, edited by Peter Mittler. *Special Educational Needs* by
R. Gulliford looks at its subject widely but selection from chapter
headings and index will enable the reader to follow the discussion
relevant to slow learners. A similar use may be made of *Living
With Handicap*, edited by E. Younghusband *et al.* J. D. Kershaw,
Handicapped Children, discusses general principles relating to
handicaps from the standpoint of a long experience as a medical
officer with a deep interest in education. His book communicates
some important insights for the teacher.

The organization of education

This is not a well-documented aspect of the education of slow learners. M. F. Cleugh, *The Slow Learner*, has a good discussion of provision and organization with emphasis on the ordinary school, though some of the legal aspects are now out of date. Chapter 1 of R. Gulliford's *Special Educational Needs*; chapter 1 of A. E. Tansley and R. Gulliford, *The Education of Slow Learning Children*; and part 3 of B. Furneaux, *The Special Child*, all discuss aspects of organization. S. Jackson, *Special Education in England and Wales*, and S. S. Segal, *No Child is Ineducable*, place the problem of educating the slow learner in the wider context of special education in general. *Slow Learners At School* has chapters on the ordinary school and remedial education whilst *Slow Learners in Secondary Schools* provides a critical survey of organization and quality in provision: both from Department of Education and Science.

The education of slow learners

There are some standard, basic books on general education. A. E. Tansley and R. Gulliford, *The Education of Slow Learning Children*, raise most of the fundamental points across the field and provide detailed guidance on approaches and methods. P. Bell, *Basic Teaching for Slow Learners*, covers the same field but is more orientated to the details of classroom practice and offers an extensive list of further reading. A. A. Williams, *Basic Subjects for Slow Learners*, deals with language, reading and mathematics, the latter in considerable detail. Spelling and writing also have detailed treatment. M. F. Cleugh, *Teaching the Slow Learner*, vols 1, 2 and 3, covers primary, secondary and special schools in a series of practical chapters written by classroom teachers. S. S. Segal, *Teaching Backward Pupils*, presents in book form reprints of articles from *Teachers' World* which pass on some useful classroom ideas. J. Duncan, *The Education of the Ordinary Child*, sets out a very special approach to education which is useful as an example of carefully constructed curricula.

There are also some useful American books. S. A. Kirk and G. O. Johnson, *Educating the Retarded Child*, sets out special class programmes at successive levels of education, includes discussion of techniques and a detailed bibliography with notes. C. P. Ingram, *The Education of the Slow-learning Child*, discusses educational objectives, sets out details of special class programmes developmentally, gives extensive summaries of units of experience in terms of planning, preparation and execution. J. H. Rothstein, *Mental Retardation*, brings together a number of important readings in the field covering all levels of education but especially strong on post-school programmes and work experience.

Special techniques

There is a growing literature in this field from which only selections can be noted. A classic book is F. J. Schonell, *Backwardness in the Basic Subjects*, an early and still valuable discussion of basic classroom techniques for pupils within normal limits of intelligence but with specific difficulties in reading, spelling and composition. A more recent, and also more general book is J. F. Reid, *Reading Problems and Practices*, which brings together readings on general reading disability, diagnosis and treatment, and preventative measures. More specific and direct is A. E. Tansley, *Reading and Remedial Reading*, which gives detailed guidance based on work with retarded readers showing visual perception difficulties. Another discussion in the same area is the Handbook to the *Look* Series, W. K. Brennan, J. M. Jackson and J. Reeves, a general discussion of visual perception difficulties in children, closely related to four pupils' books and stressing the place of motor programmes and language in remedial and preventative situations. The perceptual–motor aspects of remediation are well surveyed in P. R. Morris and H. T. A. Whiting, *Motor Impairment and Compensatory Education*, Bell, together with comprehensive references and bibliography.

Most perceptual–motor programmes seem to relate to the central book in the area, N. C. Kephart, *The Slow Learner in the Classroom*, and the associated C. M. Chaney and N. C. Kephart, *Motoric Aids to Perceptual Training*.

General surveys of special techniques will be found in D. J. Johnson and H. R. Myklebust, *Learning Disabilities*, L. Tarnopol, *Learning Disabilities*; R. M. Smith, *Clinical Teaching: Methods of Instruction for the Retarded*, McGraw-Hill (1968); and J. Francis-Williams, *Children With Specific Learning Difficulties*.

An excellent and recently published survey of the field is found in *Learning and Perceptuo–Motor Disabilities in Children*, by K. Wedell (Wiley), which summarizes the present situation, outlines the major programmes available and makes constructive suggestions of value to practical teachers. Frostig and Maslow in *Learning Problems in the Classroom* (Grune & Stratton), have provided a similar survey from a North American standpoint, summarizing general principles and discussing applications in direct relationship to basic classroom subjects.

For those readers who wish to broaden their general background *Perceptual Development in Children*, edited by A. J. Kidd and J. L. Rivoire (University of London Press), provides a good starting point. It presents seventeen studies by different authors covering the physiology of perception, perceptual development and the social, affective and cognitive aspects of perception. Though published in 1966 the book still provides a reliable and accessible introduction to its subject.

General curriculum

There is little specific British literature on the curriculum for slow learners. Teachers need to develop a general knowledge of curricular theory and apply it to their work. Useful starting-points would be: D. K. Wheeler, *Curriculum Process*, a comprehensive introduction; R. Hooper, *The Curriculum: Context, Design and Development*, Oliver and Boyd (1971), a selection of edited readings; P. H. Taylor, *'Purpose and Structure in the Curriculum'*, *Educational Review*, vols 19 and 20, pp. 159-72 and 19-29; P. H. Taylor, *Curriculum Planning for Compensatory Education*, an attempt to relate a framework to special education.

Journals

There are a number of journals which cover the field. *Special Education* is the journal of the Association of Special Education and *Forward Trends* is the journal of the Guild of Teachers of Backward Children. These journals are now amalgamated as: *Special Education: Forward Trends* the journal of the new National Council for Special Education, formed by amalgamation of the Association, the Guild and the College of Special Education. *Remedial Education* is the journal of the National Association for Remedial Education.

Bibliography

ABEL, T. M. and KINDER, E. E. (1942), *The Subnormal Adolescent Girl*, New York: Columbia University Press.

ALEXANDER, W. P. (1935), *Intelligence, concrete and abstract*, Monograph 19, *British Journal of Psychology*.

ASCHER, M. A. (1970), 'Attainments of children in ESN schools and remedial departments', *Educational Research*, 12, pp. 215-19.

ATKINSON, E. J. (1957), 'The Post-School adjustment of ESN boys', ESN Diploma dissertation, University of Birmingham.

BARON, P. A. (1938), *Backwardness in Schools*, London: Blackie.

BEARD, R. M. (1969), *An Outline of Piaget's Developmental Psychology for Students*, London: Routledge & Kegan Paul.

BELL, P. (1970), *Basic Teaching for Slow Learners*, London: Muller Educational.

BELMONT, L. and BIRCH, H. G. (1964), 'Auditory-visual integration in normal and retarded readers', *American Journal of Orthopsychiatry*, 34, 882.

BELMONT, L. and BIRCH, H. G. (1965), 'Lateral dominance, lateral awareness and reading disability', *Child Development*, 36, 57.

BENYON, S. D. (1968), *Intensive Programming for Slow Learners*, Columbus, Ohio: Merrill.

BERNSTEIN, B. (1961), 'Social structure, language and learning', *Educational Research*, 3, 163-76.

BIRCH, H. G. (ed.) (1964), *Brain Damage in Children*, New York: Williams & Wilkin.

BRENNAN, W. K. (1958), 'A Comparative Study of the Attainments, Interests, Experiences, Social Background and Social and Emotional Adjustment of Backward and Bright Boys in Industrial Lancashire, ESN Diploma dissertation, University of Birmingham.

BRENNAN, W. K. (1961), 'The Relation of Social Adaptation, Emotional Adjustment and Moral Judgement to Intelligence in Primary School Children, MEd thesis, University of Manchester.

BRENNAN, W. K. (1968), 'Education for the Outside World – Which World?', in *The Child and the Outside World*, London: National Association for Special Education (now part of the National Council for Special Education).

BRENNAN, W. K. (1970a), *The School Leavers' Workbooks*, 2nd edn, Leeds: E. J. Arnold.

BRENNAN, W. K. (1970b), 'A school leavers' programme for remedial departments', *Remedial Education*, 5, 17-21.

BRENNAN, W. K. (1971), 'A policy for remedial education', *Remedial Education*, 6, 7-11.

BRENNAN, W. K. (1972), extract from an unpublished and continuing study of the post-school adjustment of ESN school-leavers.

BRENNAN, W. K., JACKSON, J. M. and REEVES, J. (1972), *Look*, Teachers' Handbook, London: Macmillan.

BRENNER, M. W., GILLMAN, S., ZANGWILL, O. L. and FARREL, M. (1967), 'Visuo-motor ability in school children, *British Medical Journal*, 4, 259-62.

BRISON, D. W. (1967), 'Definition, diagnosis, and classification', in *Mental Retardation*, (ed.) A. A. Baumeister, Chicago: Aldine Publishing Co.

BRITISH PSYCHOLOGICAL SOCIETY (1962), 'Handicapped school-leavers', *Bulletin of the British Psychological Society*, April; 43-45.

BROWN, E. B. (1954), 'A Report on the Post-School Settlement of Birmingham Boys', ESN Diploma dissertation, University of Birmingham.

BRUNER, J. S. (1960), *The Process of Education*, Cambridge; Mass.: Harvard University Press.

BURT, SIR CYRIL (1937), *The Backward Child*, University of London Press.

BURT, SIR CYRIL (1957), *The Causes and Treatment of Backwardness*, University of London Press.

CASHDAN, A. and PUMPHREY, P. D. (1969), 'Some effects of the remedial teaching of reading', *Educational Research*, 11, 138-42.

CASHDAN, A., PUMPHREY, P. D. and LUNZER, E. A. (1971), 'Children receiving remedial teaching in reading', *Educational Research*, 13, 98-105.

CARTER, M. (1962), *Home, School and Work*, Oxford: Pergamon.

CARTER, M. (1966), *Into Work*, Harmondsworth: Penguin.

CHANEY, C. M. and KEPHART, N. C. (1968), *Motoric Aids to Perceptual Training*, Columbus, Ohio: Merrill.

CHANNING, A. (1932), *Employment of Mentally Deficient Boys and Girls*, Washington D.C.: Children's Bureau, Publication 210.

BIBLIOGRAPHY

CHAZAN, M. (1964), 'The incidence and nature of maladjustment in ESN school children', *British Journal of Educational Psychology*, 34, 292-304.

CHAZAN, M. (1967), 'The effects of remedial teaching in reading', *Remedial Education*, 2, 4-12.

CHAZAN, M. (1968), 'Inconsequential behaviour in children', *British Journal of Educational Psychology*, 38, 5-7.

CHESHIRE EDUCATION COMMITTEE, (1956), *The Education of Dull Children at the Primary Stage*, University of London Press.

CHESHIRE EDUCATION COMMITTEE, (1963), *The Education of Dull Children at the Secondary Stage*, University of London Press.

CLARK, M. M. (1970), *Reading Difficulties in Schools*, Harmondsworth: Penguin.

CLEMMENTS, R. V. (1958), *The Choice of Careers by School-children*, Manchester University Press.

CLEUGH, M. F. (ed.), (1961a), *Teaching the Slow Learner in the Primary School*, London: Methuen.

CLEUGH, M. F. (ed.) (1961b), *Teaching the Slow Learner in the Secondary School*, London: Methuen.

CLEUGH, M. F. (ed.), (1961c), *Teaching the Slow Learner in the Special School*, London: Methuen.

CLEUGH, M. F. (1968), *The Slow Learner* (2nd edn), London: Methuen.

COLLINS, J. E. (1961), *The Effects of Remedial Education*, London: Oliver & Boyd.

COLLMAN, R. D. (1956), 'Employment success of ESN ex-pupils in England', *The Slow Learning Child*, 3.

COLLMAN, R. D. and NEWLYN, D. (1956), 'Employment success of ESN ex-pupils in England', *American Journal of Mental Deficiency*, 60, 733-43.

COLLMAN, R. D. and NEWLYN, D. (1957), 'Employment success of mentally dull and intellectually normal ex-pupils in England', *American Journal of Mental Deficiency*, 61, 484-90.

CROFT, J. (1951), 'A teacher's survey of his backward class', *British Journal of Educational Psychology*, 21, 135-44.

CRUICKSHANK, W. M. (1967), *The Brain-injured Child in Home, School and Community*, New York: Syracuse University Press.

CRUICKSHANK, W. M., BENTZEN, F. A., RATZEBURG, F. E. and TANNAHAUSER, M. T. (1961), *A Teaching Method for Brain-injured Hyperactive Children*, New York: Syracuse University Press.

CUTHBERT, T. (1974), 'The N.A.R.E. national survey of remedial centres for retarded pupils', *Remedial Education*, 6, 34-6.

DAVIES, J. A. (1959), 'A Study of Interests and Attitudes of Pupils at a Secondary Modern School', MA thesis, University of Wales.

DAVIES, T. G. (1969), 'Children's Interests in a Junior School', CLD dissertation, Cambridge Institute of Education.

DE HIRSCH, K. and JANSKY, J. (1966), 'Early prediction of reading, writing and spelling ability', *British Journal of Disorders of Communication*, 1, 99-108.

DE HIRSCH, K., JANSKY, J. and LANGFORD, W. S. (1966), *Predicting Reading Failure*, New York: Harper & Row.

DEPARTMENT OF EDUCATION and SCIENCE (1963), *Half Our Future*, London: HMSO.

DEPARTMENT OF EDUCATION and SCIENCE (1964), *Slow Learners At School*, London: HMSO.

DEPARTMENT OF EDUCATION and SCIENCE (1967a), *Children and Their Primary Schools*, 2 vols, London: HMSO.

DEPARTMENT OF EDUCATION and SCIENCE (1967b), *Progress in Reading* (1948-64), London: HMSO.

DEPARTMENT OF EDUCATION and SCIENCE (1971), *Slow Learners in Secondary Schools*, London: HMSO.

DEPARTMENT OF EDUCATION and SCIENCE (1972), *Children With Reading Difficulties*, London: HMSO.

DEPARTMENT OF EDUCATION and SCIENCE (1973), *Statistics of Education: Schools*, London: HMSO.

DESCOEUDRES, A. (1928), *The Education of Mentally Defective Children*, London: Harrap.

DIMICHAEL, S. G. (1950), *Vocational Rehabilitation of the Mentally Retarded*, Washington D.C.: Government Printing Office.

DOUGLAS, J. W. B. (1964), *The Home and the School*, London: MacGibbon & Kee.

DOUGLAS, J. W. B., ROSS, J. M. and SIMPSON, H. R. (1968), *All Our Future*, London: Peter Davies.

DUNCAN, J. (1942), *The Education of the Ordinary Child*, London: Nelson.

DUROJAIYE, M. O. A. (1969), 'Occupational choice and special education of educationally subnormal children', *British Journal of Educational Psychology*, 39, 88-9.

FEATHERSTONE, W. B. (1951), *Teaching the Slow Learner*, New York: Bureau of Publications, Teachers' College, Columbia University.

FERGUSON, T. and CUNNISON, J. (1951), *The Young Wage-Earner*, London: Oxford University Press.

FLAVELL, J. C. (1963), *The Developmental Psychology of Jean Piaget*, Princetown, N.J.: Van Nostrand.

FLEMMING, C. M., DIGARIA, D. F. and NEWTH, H. R. G. (1960), 'Preferences and values amongst adolescent boys and girls', *Educational*

Research, 3, 221-4.

FRANCIS-WILLIAMS, J. (1970), *Children With Specific Learning Difficulties*, Oxford: Pergamon.

FRANSELLA, F. and GREVER, D. (1966), 'Multiple regression equations for predicting reading age from chronological age and WISC verbal I.Q.', *British Journal of Educational Psychology*, 35, 86-9.

FROSTIG, M. and HORNE, D. (1967), *Handbook to The Frostig Programme for the Development of Visual Perception*, Chicago: Follett.

FROSTIG, M. and MASLOW, P. (1973), *Learning Problems in the Classroom*, New York: Grune & Stratton.

FURNEAUX, B. (1969), *The Special Child*, Harmondsworth: Penguin.

GALLAGHER, J. J. (1960), *The Tutoring of Brain-Injured Mentally Retarded Children*, Springfield, Ill.: Thomas.

GOLDSTEIN, H. (1964), 'Social and occupational adjustment', in *Mental Retardation: A Review of Research*, (ed.) H. A. Stevens and R. Heber. University of Chicago Press.

GOLDSTEIN, H. and HEBER, R. (1967), 'Preparation of mentally retarded youth for gainful employment', in *Mental Retardation*, (ed.) J. H. Rothstein, New York: Holt, Rinehart & Winston.

GOLDSTEIN, H. and SEIGLE, D. (1958), *A Curriculum Guide for Teachers of the Educable Mentally Handicapped*, Springfield: Illinois Department of Public Instruction.

GORDON, N. (1969), 'Helping the clumsy child in school', *Special Education*, 58, 19-20.

GREEN, L. F. (1969), 'Comparison of school attainments', *Special Education*, 58, 7-12.

GULLIFORD, R. (1969), *Backwardness and Educational Failure*, Slough: National Foundation for Educational Research.

GULLIFORD, R. (1971), *Special Educational Needs*, London: Routledge & Kegan Paul.

HAMMOND, D. (1948), *Times Educational Supplement*, 14 August.

HAMMOND, D. (1963), *Times Educational Supplement*, 26 July.

HAMMOND, D. (1967), 'Reading attainment in the primary schools of Brighton', *Educational Research*, 10, 57-64.

HARGROVE, A. L. (1954), *The Social Adaptation of ESN School Leavers*, London: National Association for Mental Health.

HART, W. J. (1969), 'The Case for a Learning Centre at a Day Special School for ESN Pupils', Diploma dissertation, University of Bristol Institute of Education.

HEREFORD, M. E. M. (1957), *Youth at Work: The Future Develop-*

ment of the Youth Employment Service, London: HMSO.

HIGHFIELD, M. E. (1951), *The Education of Backward Children*, London: Harrap. (Revised edn of Hill, 1939.)

HILL, M. E. (1939), *The Education of Backward Children*, London: Harrap. (See Highfield, 1951.)

HOWLETT, G. F. (1968), 'Key Essentials for ESN School Leavers', Dip. Ed dissertation, University of Nottingham.

HUNGERFORD, R. H., DEPROSPO, C. J. and ROSENZWEIG, L. E. (1948), 'The non-academic pupil', in *Philosophy of Occupational Education*, (ed.) R. H. Hungerford, New York: Association for Teachers of Special Education.

HUNT, J. MCV. (1961), *Intelligence and Experience*, New York: Ronald Press.

HUNT, J. MCV. (1967), 'The Psychological Basis for Using Pre-School Enrichment as an Antidote for Cultural Deprivation', in *Education of the Disadvantaged* (ed.) A. H. Passow, M. Goldberg and A. J. Tannenbaum, New York: Holt, Rinehart & Winston.

INGRAM, C. (1960), *The Education of the Slow-Learning Child*, (1st edn 1953), New York: Ronald Press.

INGRAM, T. T. S. (1960), 'Paediatric aspects of specific developmental dysphasia, dyslexia and dysgraphia', *Cerebral Palsy Bulletin*, 2, 254-76.

INGRAM, T. T. S. (1964), 'Late and Poor Talkers', in *The Child Who Does Not Talk*, (ed.) C. Renfrew and K. Murphy, London: Heinemann.

INGRAM, T. T. S. (1971), 'Specific learning difficulties in childhood: a medical point of view', *British Journal of Educational Psychology*, 41, 6-15.

INNER LONDON EDUCATION AUTHORITY (1968), *Home and School*, London: ILEA.

INNER LONDON EDUCATION AUTHORITY (1969), *Literacy Survey*, London: ILEA.

INNER LONDON EDUCATION AUTHORITY (1969), *Children With Special Difficulties*, London: ILEA.

INSKEEP, A. D. (1926), *Teaching Dull and Retarded Children*, New York: Macmillan.

JACKSON, R. N. (1966), 'How reliable are follow-ups?', *Special Education*, 55, 4-6.

JACKSON, R. N. (1968), 'Employment and Adjustment of Educable Mentally Handicapped School Leavers', in *The Child and the Outside World*, London: National Association for Special Education (now part of The National Council for Special Education).

JACKSON, R. N. (1970), 'Educable mental handicap and delinquency', *Educational Research*, 12, 128-34.

JACKSON, S. (1966), *Special Education in England and Wales*, London: Oxford University Press.

JACKSON, S. (1968), *A Teacher's Guide to Tests and Testing*, London: Longman.

JERROLD, M. A. and FOX, R. (1968), 'Pre-jobs for the boys', *Special Education*, 57, 15-18.

JERROLD, M. A. and FOX, R. (1971), 'The preparation of immature and educationally subnormal school leavers for working life', *Forward Trends*, 15, 73-5.

JOHNSON, D. J. and MYKLEBUST, H. R. (1967), *Learning Disabilities: Educational Principles and Practices*, New York: Grune & Stratton.

JOHNSON, G. O. (1968), 'The Education of the Mentally Retarded', in *Education of Exceptional Children and Youth*, (2nd edn), (ed.) W. J. Cruickshank and G. O. Johnson, London: Staples.

JONES, C. (1970), 'A study of retarded boys', CLD Diploma dissertation, Cambridge Institute of Education.

JONES, C. H. (1970), 'The Delves School "Work Experience" Project', *Remedial Education*, 5, 22-3.

JONES, D. J. (1957), 'A Study of the Problems and Needs of Boys who left a Residential School for ESN Children', ESN Diploma dissertation, University of Birmingham.

KENNEDY, R. J. R. (1948), *The Social Adjustment of Morons in a Connecticut City*, Hartford, Conn.: Social Services Department.

KEPHART, N. C. (1960), *The Slow Learner in the Classroom*, (2nd edn 1971), Columbus, Ohio: Merrill.

KERSHAW, J. D. (1961), *Handicapped Children*, London: Heinemann.

KIRK, S. A. (1964), 'Research in Education', in *Mental Retardation*, (ed.) H. A. Stevens and R. Heber, University of Chicago Press.

KIRK, S. A. and JOHNSON, G. O. (1951), *Educating the Retarded Child*, Cambridge, Mass.: Houghton Mifflin.

KNIGHT, D. J. and WALKER, M. A. (1965), 'A factory day at school', *Special Education*, 54, 7-9.

LAWRENCE, D. J. (1969), 'Interests of Young Secondary Modern Pupils', CLD Diploma dissertation, Cambridge Institute of Education.

LAWTON, D. (1968), *Social Class, Language and Education*, London: Routledge & Kegan Paul.

LAWTON, D. (1970), 'Preparation for Changes in the Curriculum', in *The Extra Year*, (ed.) J. W. Tibble, London: Routledge & Kegan Paul.

LORD, A. B. (1933), 'A survey of four hundred and forty-nine special class pupils', *Journal of Educational Research*, 2, 108-14.

LOVELL, K. (1966), 'The Aetiology of Reading Failure', in *The First International Reading Symposium, Oxford 1964*, (ed.) J. Downing, London: Cassell.

LOVELL, K. (1968), 'Backwardness and Retardation', in *Educational Research in Britain*, (ed.) H. J. Butcher, University of London Press.

LOVELL, K. and GORTON, A. (1968), 'A study of some differences between backward and normal readers of average intelligence', *British Journal of Educational Psychology*, 38, 240-8.

LOVELL, K., GRAY, E. and OLIVER, D. E. (1964), 'A further study of some cognitive and other disabilities in backward readers of average non-verbal reasoning scores', *British Journal of Educational Psychology*, 34, 275-9.

LOVELL, K., SHAPTON, D. and WARREN, N. S. (1964), 'A study of some cognitive and other disabilities in backward readers of average intelligence as assessed by a non-verbal test', *British Journal of Educational Psychology*, 34, 58-64.

LOVELL, K., WHITE, C. and WHITLEY, R. (1965), 'Studying backward readers', *Special Education*, 54, 9-13.

LOVETT, C. J. (1966), 'Post-School Adjustment of ESN Children', DipEd dissertation, University of Nottingham.

MAIZELLS, J. (1965), 'The Entry of School Leavers into Employment', *British Journal of Industrial Relations*, March.

MARSTON, N. and STOTT, D. H. (1970), 'Inconsequence as a primary type of behaviour disturbance in children', *British Journal of Educational Psychology*, 40, 15-20.

MARTENS, E. H. (1950), *Curriculum Adjustment for the Mentally Retarded* (revised edn), Washington, D.C.: Government Printing Office.

MATTHEW, G. C. (1963), 'The Post-School Social Adaptation of Educationally Subnormal Boys', MEd thesis, University of Manchester.

MATTHEW, G. C. (1964), 'The social competence of the subnormal school leaver', *Journal of Mental Subnormality*, 10, 83-8.

MATTHEW, G. C. (1968), 'The Post-school Adaptation of ESN Boys', in *The Child and the Outside World*, London: National Association for Special Education (now part of the National Council for Special Education).

BIBLIOGRAPHY

MAYS, J. B. (1962), *Education and the Urban Child*, University of Liverpool Press.

MINISTRY OF EDUCATION (1937), *The Education of Backward Children*, London: HMSO (reprinted 1949).

MINISTRY OF EDUCATION (1946), *Special Educational Treatment*, London: HMSO.

MINISTRY OF EDUCATION (1959), *Handicapped Pupils and School Health Regulations*, London: HMSO.

MORRIS, J. M. (1966), *Standards and Progress in Reading*, Slough: National Foundation for Educational Research.

MORRIS, J. M. (1969), *Reading in the Primary School*, London: Newnes.

MORRIS, P. R. and WHITING, H. T. A. (1971), *Motor Impairment and Compensatory Education*, London: Bell.

NATIONAL ASSOCIATION FOR REMEDIAL EDUCATION (1970), *Report of the Working Party on Remedial Education*, London: National Association for Remedial Education.

NATIONAL ASSOCIATION OF TEACHERS OF ENGLISH (1969), 'Reading survey by Warwickshire NATE', (ed) J. I. Ellis, *English in Education*, 3, 1, 31-6.

NATIONAL EDUCATION ASSOCIATION (1938), *The Purpose of Education in American Democracy*, Washington, D.C.: Government Printing Office.

NICKELL, V. (1951), *Educating the Mentally Handicapped in the Secondary School*, Springfield, Ill.: Department of Public Instruction.

O'CONNOR, N. (1954), 'Defectives working in the community', *American Journal of Mental Deficiency*, 59, 173-80.

PAUL, L. (1962), *The Transition from School to Work*, London: Industrial Welfare Society.

PHELPS, H. (1956), 'Post-school adjustment of mentally retarded children in selected Ohio cities', *Exceptional Children*, 23, 58-62.

PHILLIPS, C. J. (1961), 'On Comparing Scores from Tests of Attainment with Scores from Tests of Ability in order to obtain Indices of Retardation by Differences or Ratios', thesis, University of Birmingham Institute of Education.

PRINGLE, M. L. KELLMER, BUTLER, N. R. and DAVIE, R. (1966), *11,000 Seven-Year-Olds*, London: Longman.

RAVENETTE, A. T. (1970), 'Culturally handicapped children', in *Assessment of Mental and Physical Handicaps*, (ed.) P. Mittler, London: Methuen.

REID, J. F. (1970), 'Reading', in *Educational Research in Britain*, (ed.) H. J. Butcher, University of London Press.

ROACH, E. G. and KEPHART, N. C. (1966), *The Purdue Perceptual-Motor Survey*, Columbus, Ohio: Merrill.

ROBINSON, H. B. and ROBINSON, N. M. (1965), *The Mentally Retarded Child* (2nd edn), New York: McGraw-Hill.

ROTHSTEIN, J. H. (1967), *Mental Retardation*, New York: Holt, Rinehart & Winston.

RUTTER, M. (1966), 'Severe Reading Retardation, Epilepsy, Maladjustment and Neurological Disorders', in *What is Special Education?*, London: National Association for Special Education (now part of the National Council for Special Education).

RUTTER, M., TIZARD, J. and WHITMORE, K. (1970), *Education, Health and Behaviour*, London: Longman.

SAMPSON, O. C. (1969), 'Remedial education services', *Remedial Education*, 4, 3-8 and 61-5.

SAMPSON, O. C. and PUMPHREY, P. D. (1970), 'A study of remedial education in the secondary stage of schooling', *Remedial Education*, 5, 102-11.

SANDERS, C. (1948), 'Insecurity and maladjustment in children', *British Journal of Educational Psychology*, 18, 148-55.

SAVAGE, R. D. (1968), *Psychometric Assessment of the Individual Child*, Harmondsworth: Penguin.

SAVAGE, R. D. and O'CONNOR, D. (1966), 'The assessment of reading and arithmetic retardation in school', *British Journal of Educational Psychology*, 34, 317-18.

SCOTTISH COUNCIL FOR RESEARCH IN EDUCATION (1953), *Social Implications of the 1947 Scottish Mental Survey*, University of London Press.

SCHONELL, F. J. (1942), *Backwardness in the Basic Subjects*, London: Oliver & Boyd.

SCHONELL, F. J. (1949), 'The development of educational research in Britain', *British Journal of Educational Psychology*, 19, 82-99.

SCHONELL, F. J. (1957), *Diagnosis and Remedial Teaching in Arithmetic*, London: Oliver & Boyd.

SCHOOLS COUNCIL (n.d.), *Science for the Young School Leaver*, London: Schools Council.

SCHOOLS COUNCIL (1965), *Raising the School Leaving Age*, London: HMSO.

SCHOOLS COUNCIL (1967a), *Society and the Young School Leaver*, London: HMSO.

SCHOOLS COUNCIL (1967b), *Mathematics for the Majority*, London: HMSO.

SCHOOLS COUNCIL (1967c), *The Educational Implications of Social and Economic Change*, London: HMSO.

SCHOOLS COUNCIL (1970a), *Cross'd With Adversity*, London: Evans/Methuen Educational.

SCHOOLS COUNCIL (1970b), *Curriculum Planning for Compensatory Education*, London: Schools Council.

SCHOOLS COUNCIL (1971), *Choosing a Curriculum for the Young School Leaver*, London: Evans/Methuen Educational.

SEGAL, S. S. (1963), *Teaching Backward Pupils*, London: Evans.

SEGAL, S. S. (1967), *No Child Is Ineducable*, Oxford: Pergamon.

SKINNER, W. G. (1970), 'Link Courses in Colleges of Further Education', University of Keele (unpublished).

START, K. B. and WELLS, B. K. (1972), *The Trend of Reading Standards*, Slough: National Foundation for Educational Research.

STEVENS, G. D. (1958), 'An analysis of objectives for the education of children with retarded mental development', *American Journal of Mental Deficiency*, 63, 225-35, also reprinted as chapter 24 in Rothstein (1967).

STOTT, D. H. (1963), *The Social Adjustment of Children* (4th edn, 1971), University of London Press.

STOTT, D. H. (1966), *Studies of Troublesome Children*, London: Tavistock Publications.

STRAUSS, A. A. and LEHTINEN, L. E. (1947), *Psychopathology and Education of the Brain-Injured Child*, New York: Grune & Stratton.

STRAUSS, A. A. and KEPHART, N. C. (1955), *Psychopathology and Education of the Brain-Injured Child*, vol. 2, New York: Grune & Stratton.

TABA, H. (1962), *Curriculum Development: Theory and Practice*, New York: Harcourt, Brace & World.

TANSLEY, A. E. (1967), *Reading and Remedial Reading*, London: Routledge & Kegan Paul.

TANSLEY, A. E. and BRENNAN, W. K. (1963), *Teacher's Book to School Leavers' Handbook* (2nd edn, 1971), Leeds: E. J. Arnold.

TANSLEY, A. E. and GULLIFORD, R. (1960), *The Education of Slow Learning Children*, London: Routledge & Kegan Paul.

TARNOPOL, L. (1969), *Learning Disabilities: Introduction to Educational and Medical Management*, Springfield, Ill.: Thomas.

TAYLOR, G. A. (1957), 'An After-Care Follow-Up of School Leavers', ESN Diploma dissertation, University of Birmingham.

TAYLOR, P. H. (1967), 'Purpose and structure in the curriculum', *Educational Review*, 19, 159-72 and 20, 19-29.

TAYLOR, P. H. (1970), *Curriculum Planning for Compensatory Education: A Suggested Procedure*, London: Schools Council.

TUCKEY, L., PARFIT, J. and TUCKEY, B. (1973), *Handicapped School-Leavers*, Windsor: National Foundation for Educational Research.

TYSON, M. (1963), 'A pilot study of remedial visuo-motor training', *Special Education*, 52, 22-5.

TYSON, M. (1970), 'The design of remedial programmes', in *The Psychological Assessment of Mental and Physical Handicaps*, (ed.) P. Mittler, London: Methuen.

VENESS, T. (1962), *School Leavers – Their Aspirations and Expectations*, London: Methuen.

VERNON, P. E. (1960), *Intelligence and Attainment Tests*, University of London Press.

WEDELL, K. (1968), 'Perceptual-motor difficulties', *Special Education*, 57, 25-30.

WEDELL, K. (1974), *Learning and Perceptuo–Motor Disabilities in Children*, New York: Wiley.

WHEELER, D. K. (1967), *Curriculum Process*, University of London Press.

WILLIAMS, A. A. (1970), *Basic Subjects for Slow Learners*, London: Methuen.

WILLIAMS, P. (1965), 'The ascertainment of ESN Children', *Educational Research*, 7, 136-46.

WILLIAMS, P. (1970), 'Slow-learning Children and Educational Problems', in *The Psychological Assessment of Mental and Physical Handicaps*, ed. P. Mittler, London: Methuen.

WILLIAMS, P. and GRUBER, E. (1967), *Response to Special Schooling*, London: Longman.

WILSON, J. (1971), 'A Study of the Occupational Adjustment of Backward Boys and Girls', MEd thesis, University of Leicester.

WILSON, M. D. (1953), 'The vocational preferences of secondary modern school children, *British Journal of Educational Psychology*, 23, 97-113 and 163-79.

WISEMAN, S. (1964), *Education and Environment*, Manchester University Press.

WISEMAN, S. (1968), 'Educational Deprivation and Disadvantage', in *Educational Research in Britain*, (ed.) H. J. Butcher, University of London Press.

WOLFENSBERGER, W. (1967), 'Vocational Preparation and Occupation', in *Mental Retardation*, (ed.) A. Baumeister, Chicago: Aldine.

WYMAN, G. C. (1968), 'A Study of the Post-School Adjustment of Slow Learners from a Secondary Modern School', CLD Diploma dissertation, Cambridge Institute of Education.

BIBLIOGRAPHY

YOUNGHUSBAND, E., BIRCHALL, D., DAVIE, R. and PRINGLE, M. L. K. (1970), *Living With Handicap,* London: National Bureau for Co-operation in Child Care.